HYBRID**PICKING**
GUITARTECHNIQUE

Master the Techniques, Secrets & Versatility of Modern Hybrid Picking on Guitar

LEVI**CLAY**

FUNDAMENTAL**CHANGES**

Hybrid Picking Guitar Technique

Master the Techniques, Secrets & Versatility of Modern Hybrid Picking on Guitar

ISBN: 978-1-78933-248-3

Published by **www.fundamental-changes.com**

www.fundamental-changes.com

Over 13,000 fans on Facebook: **FundamentalChangesInGuitar**

Instagram: **FundamentalChanges**

For over 350 Free Guitar Lessons with Videos Check Out

www.fundamental-changes.com

Cover Image Copyright: Lee Wrathe, Ibanez UK, used by permission

Contents

Introduction

Welcome to my book devoted to developing fluid and musical hybrid picking technique. Congratulations on taking this step to move your guitar playing skills to the next level.

Hybrid picking refers to the skill of combining pick technique with the other fingers of the picking hand to offer more options for striking the strings. While it's a technique more common in genres such as Country and Blues, you'll get the most from it if you treat it like any other aspect of your guitar playing. It can work with any style and, once you integrate it into your playing, you may find that it becomes part of your day-to-day approach to your instrument.

The history of hybrid picking is difficult to chart. There is no way to say for certain when it was introduced and, for many, it's just a common sense approach. We know that long before the popularisation of modern steel string and electric guitars, the guitar was played with gut strings in a more classical style. There are numerous texts dating back hundreds of years, such as Mauro Giuliani's *120 Right Hand Studies* and Francisco Tarrega's *Complete Technical Studies,* that showcase the long history of using the fingers to pluck the strings, and the pedagogy surrounding the subject.

Many early guitar players came from a classical background (since this was the only way to get a formal education), and others moved to the guitar from instruments like the banjo. This meant that as flat-picking became the predominant style of the 1920s, the dexterity developed for fingerstyle naturally inspired ideas that could be used in combination with the pick.

I also studied classical guitar in my formative years, as it was the only formal instruction offered by my school. While I spent my lessons working on "correct" technique, outside of school I wanted to be in a rock band and I wasn't about to throw away my pick. So, I would spend time trying to play my classical pieces with the pick in my hand, so it was there if I needed it. While my teachers briefly entertained this approach, they were adamant it wouldn't be of much use to me. Well, Messrs Brown and Johnson, I humbly suggest I've had the last laugh there!

As my playing developed, I discovered many guitarists who used hybrid picking in their playing – from the ferocious picking of Zakk Wylde and John 5, to the delicate chordal ideas of Eric Johnson and Tommy Emmanuel. Then there was the Rockabilly stylings of Brian Setzer and James Burton, to the all-out insanity of Danny Gatton and Bumblefoot. And, of course, Brett Garsed, Brent Mason, Johnny Hiland and Buckethead. I realised that hybrid picking was a technique I could apply to whatever I wanted, rather than it being something that put me in a box. Now *that* was exciting!

When it comes to technique education, instruction for the guitar is sadly lacking, compared to an instrument like the piano, which has hundreds of years of evolution behind it. Respected educators from all over the world still argue about the correct posture for playing guitar, sowing confusion and doubt among their students.

That's not to say there have been *no* good resources for hybrid picking (the works of Gustavo Assis-Brasil are particularly excellent), but I wanted to see a book suited to the beginner-to-intermediate hybrid picker that would be more useful than material even I find challenging after 20 years of practice!

Why learn hybrid picking?

There are three key reasons why it will help you to develop a solid hybrid picking technique.

Physical Reasons

Hybrid picking can be used to perform musical ideas that are difficult (or impossible) with the pick. For example, using a finger to pluck a note on the 2nd string right after a picked note on the 5th string is easy with hybrid picking. The hardest aspect of standard picking technique has always been string-crossing mechanics, but hybrid picking reduces the pressure in your picking hand and results in effortless speed for technical passages.

Tonal Reasons

With work, a hybrid-picked note *can* sound almost identical to a picked note. More normally though, notes played with the fingers will sound quite different to picked notes. This is a good thing and provides a wonderful tonal variation that many players take full advantage of, adding some spank to certain notes. You'll hear this idea used frequently in Country and Southern Rock influenced playing.

Hybrid picking can also enhance your chord playing. You don't have to be limited to the strumming sound you're accustomed to; now you can use the pick and fingers to sound notes simultaneously, more like a piano player.

Playing Health

Playing a musical instrument is an extremely demanding task for the body and that's hard to ignore. I've been playing guitar for 20 years now, and much of that time has been spent developing my shred guitar technique. I've been relatively lucky, as I'm still playing all these years on, but I've seen many of my peers develop serious physical conditions such as Repetitive Strain Injury, Carpal Tunnel Syndrome and even Tennis Elbow.

Combining guitar playing with my job at a PC, working as a music transcriber, isn't without its physical challenges, so hybrid picking is essential for me now. It requires almost no movement from the wrist, forearm or elbow, so it's the least physically strenuous way for me to play the instrument.

What's ahead...

This book is structured in a way that gradually introduces more challenging exercises as you progress. Regardless of your playing ability, I recommend you begin at Chapter One, where we'll talk in depth about the mechanics of hybrid picking. Fully mastering this section will help you to progress through the rest of the material at a decent pace, with the fundamentals in place.

From there, we'll move on to string crossing, alternate picking with hybrid picking, using multiple fingers for double-stops and rolls, and beyond. All you need is a guitar, your pick and your fingers!

While some players take a disciplined approach to nail maintenance to create a pick-like tone, I have no nails on my picking hand, so there are no special nail growing requirements to play anything in this book.

As with anything in music, your ears always trump your eyes. Careful attention has gone into every one of the audio recordings accompanying this book, so it's important to listen to them in detail. We're not just looking to play the right notes – we want them to sound right too.

I recorded all the examples on my Fender Telecaster with a medium pointed V-Pick, through my Kemper profiling amp using a selection of different profiles. Most had some delay and reverb added, along with some subtle compression, just to help bring out those finger-picked notes.

Hybrid picking notation is pretty non-standard and there is no consensus on how it should be written, so for clarification I'll be using the PIMAC notation conventions.

P = *pulgar* (thumb)

I = *indice* (index or first finger)

M = *medio* (middle finger)

A = *anular* (ring finger)

C = *chico* (pinkie finger)

As you'll be holding the pick with the thumb and index finger, you won't come across any "P" or "I" instructions, but other fingerings are marked below the notation throughout, for maximum detail.

Get the Audio

The audio files for this book are available to download for free from **www.fundamental-changes.com.** The link is in the top right-hand corner. Click on the "Guitar" link then simply select this book title from the drop-down menu and follow the instructions to get the audio.

We recommend that you download the files directly to your computer, not to your tablet, and extract them there before adding them to your media library. You can then put them onto your tablet, iPod or burn them to CD. On the download page there are instructions and we also provide technical support via the contact form.

Get the audio and over 350 free guitar lessons with videos check out:

www.fundamental-changes.com

Join our active Facebook community:

www.facebook.com/groups/fundamentalguitar

Tag us for a share on Instagram: **FundamentalChanges**

Chapter One – Position, Motion & Adjacent Strings

The first thing you need to do when learning hybrid picking is to get to grips with the physical motions.

Let's start with the pick.

It's important to hold the pick between the thumb and index finger only, so you have the maximum number of fingers free to pick the strings. I mention this up front because there some players who hold the pick between the thumb and middle finger, which severely reduces picking potential. While nothing is set in stone, using the thumb and index finger adds much more versatility.

Now let's look at the finger assignments.

I want you to place your pick on the 5th string, then rest your middle, ring and pinkie fingers on the 4th, 3rd and 2nd, strings respectively.

Notice that the fingers don't sit perfectly in line with one another, so that they're parallel to the frets or neck pickup. Instead, they create a natural angle of about 45 degrees across each string. As your pick rests on the string, your middle finger will be a little closer to the bridge, the ring will be closer still, and so on.

Your palm should be located by the bridge, ready to palm mute, and there should be no bend in the wrist, so you could draw a straight line from your elbow to your knuckles.

Take some time to remove and replace your hand, with the fingers on each string and the pick resting on the 5th string, so that you get used to automatically going to this position. Think of this as your resting position, or as "pre-placement" before playing.

Now let's talk about plucking a note with the middle finger.

If the finger has been correctly pre-placed, it is already in contact with the string. It's ready to go and all you need to do is lift the finger towards you to sound a note.

Hold down the 5th fret on the D string and pick it a few times with your middle finger. The secret here is that the motion does *not* come from the wrist. Don't lift your hand up at all, just pluck the string with the motion of the finger itself. It's possible (but not essential) to pluck with the middle finger without the pick even leaving the A string.

Notice that the plucking motion comes from *closing* the hand. The note is plucked, then the finger is immediately placed back on the string ready to pluck again.

Example 1a:

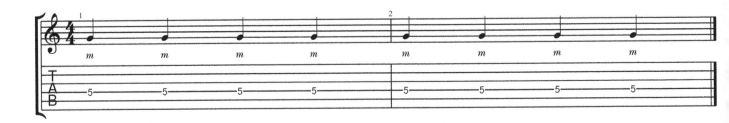

Now let's pick the G string with the middle finger. We'll do so by moving the whole position of the hand over one string, so that the pick now sits on the D (4th) string while you're playing the G string, and the other two fingers sit on the B and high E strings. Remember that the movement of the hand comes from the elbow, rather than the wrist.

Example 1b:

What you'll notice immediately is that the notes sound clear and distinct. This is due to the *plane* on which you pick the string. Your finger comes from the underside of the string and sounds the note by pulling the string away from the guitar. This means that if you pick the string with any force, it will slap back against the frets and create a more distinct sound – the aforementioned "spank".

In the following example, pick the same note but increase the pluck velocity from soft all the way up to a spanking Country sound. This can be heard clearly on the audio track.

Note that the harder you pluck, the more the motion starts to come from pulling the whole hand away from the guitar, rather than just the one finger.

Example 1c:

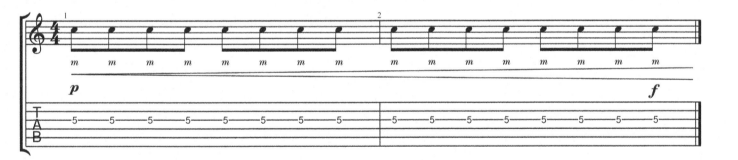

Now we'll look how to alternate between the pick and one finger.

We'll start by examining one mechanic: using the middle finger to pluck a note on the string adjacent to the pick. In this example, the pick is on the D string, so the middle finger plucks the G string.

I play this example in free time, beginning slow and picking up speed (which is a hugely effective method for developing your speed).

Example 1d:

Next, use the pick to pluck the G string, and the middle finger to pluck the B string. The motion is the same, the only difference is that your hand has repositioned a little closer to the ground.

Example 1e:

It doesn't matter where your hand is, the distance between the pick and fingers always feels the same. In this next example, place your pick on the A string, so your middle finger is primed to pluck the D string.

Example 1f:

With this motion under your fingers, it's time to play something that sounds less like an exercise and more like a lick.

This example introduces the common movement of a pull-off to an open string. Pluck the string with the middle finger, then pull off to the open G string. Repeat this motion before using the pick to strike the D string.

Example 1g:

The beauty of this idea is that it can easily be moved around the neck, while the mechanics of the picking hand remain the same.

Move the pattern down three frets and it starts to sound more like a Country rock lick using the A Major Pentatonic scale.

Example 1h:

Here's another idea that focuses on alternating between the pick and middle finger, but now on the B and E strings. This kind of idea could be heard on anything from the Allman Brother Band to AC/DC, but it's a great exercise. Pick the second string and pluck the first.

Example 1i:

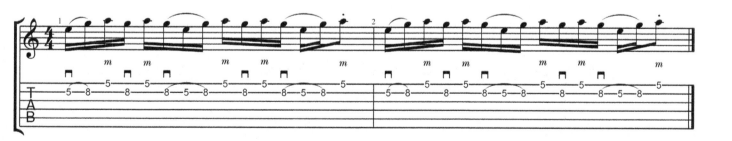

The next example adds another picked downstroke in a similar exercise.

This time, you'll play a picked downstroke on the B string, pull off, then move the pick over to the G string for another downstroke. Once this is done, the middle finger is primed to pluck the B string before repeating the same motif again.

The idea here is that it's much more efficient to use a finger to pluck the note the second time than it is to move the pick over to play an upstroke.

Example 1j:

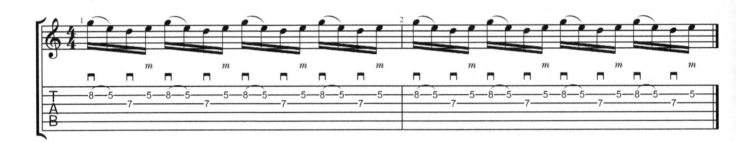

Now you're starting to develop a bit of comfort moving across strings, here's a short repeating mechanic with the pick moving from the G string to the D, then using the middle finger on that G string instead of the pick.

Example 1k:

Here's that same mechanic applied to a full lick made famous by Brad Paisley. Be careful with the string crossing on this one as it can easily trip you up at speed.

Example 1l:

The following example introduces a bend. This is one of the best places to use hybrid picking, as alternating between two strings should now be a breeze.

If you're struggling to finger this, try using the pinkie finger on the 8th fret, and the index and middle together on the 7th fret for support when bending.

Example 1m:

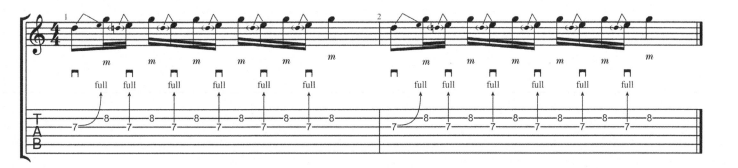

One way to look at these early hybrid picking examples is that you're using the middle finger to substitute for a picked upstroke. At speed, this just feels like you're alternating between the pick and finger, much like alternate picking.

To practice this idea, let's apply this string crossing mechanic to an A minor triad. Start by picking the notes on the D and B strings with downstrokes, before filling in the middle string with your middle finger.

The idea behind this exercise is to help you get used to moving the picking hand after a finger pluck.

Example 1n:

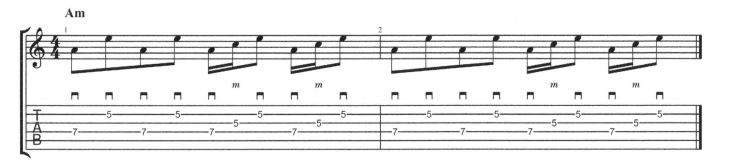

Here's that same mechanic applied to a chord progression in A minor.

The picking hand doesn't do anything new here, you just need to focus on moving the fretting hand between chords. Remember, only use your pick and middle finger!

Example 1o:

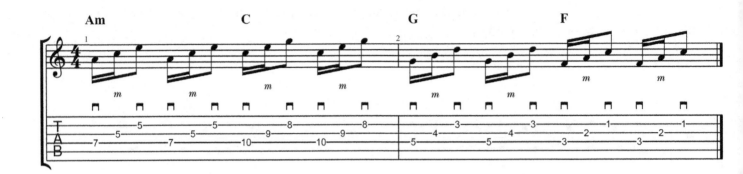

Let's expand on this idea and begin to move the picking pattern between the D, G and B string group and the G, B and E string group. As with the previous example, the hybrid picking motion doesn't change, you now just need to move your hand across the strings.

Example 1p:

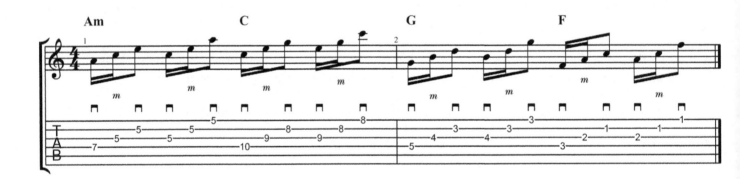

Now you're getting the feel for moving the pick immediately after plucking with the middle finger, let's fill in the gaps in the rhythm with some ascending four-note arpeggios across the same chord progression.

This ascending four-note pattern is built from two adjacent pairs of strings, the D and G strings, then the B and E.

This feels awkward at first, but when you compare it to alternate picking across multiple strings, you'll see how low effort this approach is. Again, remember that you're only using your pick and middle fingers.

Example 1q:

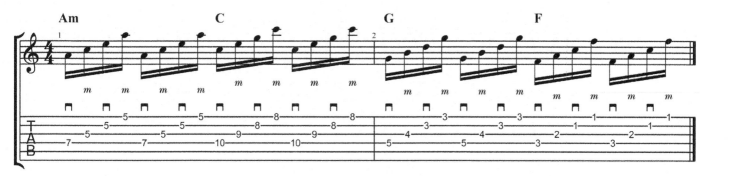

This hybrid motion can be applied to any chord progression, so I'd encourage you to get creative and think of your own sequences to program the technique into muscle memory. To get you going, this example contains the same chords as before, but now using different voicings for the G and F chords.

Example 1r:

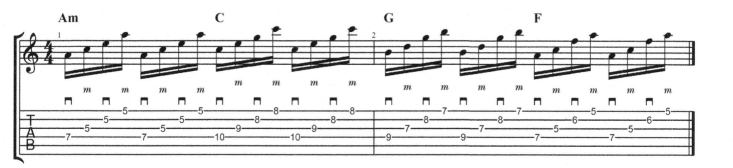

Now that you're getting a feel for the pick and middle finger working in tandem, I want to close this chapter with some challenging little alternating exercises.

One of my biggest influences has always been Brent Mason. While Brent is a Country player, it's hard to describe his approach as real hybrid picking because he uses a thumb pick and fingers. The thumb pick means that for fast scalar runs, he needs to alternate between the pick and fingers.

Applying this idea to a scale may feel tricky at first because the pick and finger often have to play the same string. As a primer, let's begin by alternating between pick and finger on just one note.

Example 1s:

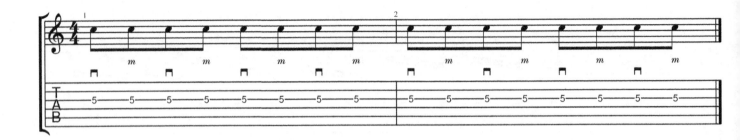

This motion can be moved between strings, as shown in the following exercise.

Example 1t:

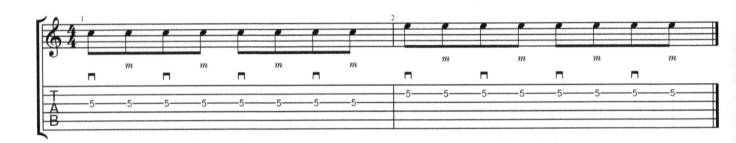

Now you're ready to apply this to a full scale. I recommend saying "pick, finger, pick, finger" out loud as you play. Sooner or later, this motion will feel completely automatic, it just takes time.

Example 1u:

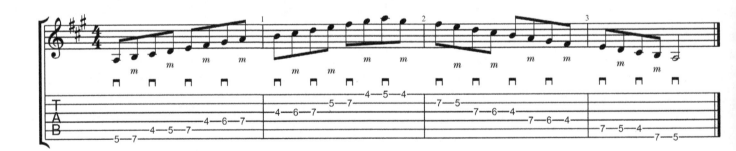

Now, to give your hand a full workout, play the same scale fingering with the same alternating motion, but this time begin with the middle finger.

Example 1v:

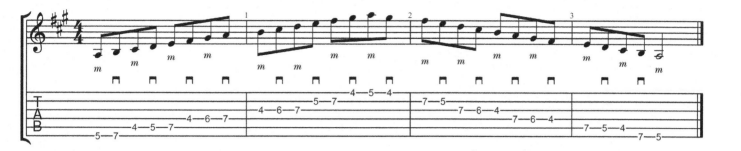

Seven-note scales are a great workout for this mechanic because the number of notes isn't consistent across each string. This means that you'll have to change strings with both pick and finger.

As pentatonic scales normally have two notes per string, the string crossing mechanic is more consistent.

When you ascend a pentatonic scale beginning with a picked note, each string will start with the pick.

Example 1w:

If you reverse this pattern, each string starts with a middle finger pluck.

Example 1x:

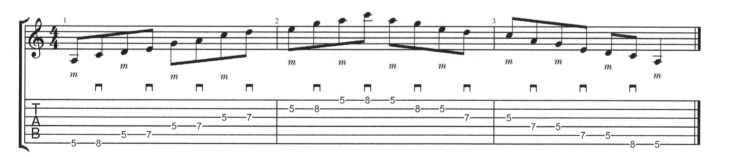

Applying this motion to arpeggios creates another technical challenge, as you must often execute single notes on strings before moving to another. This requires focus, but becomes automatic with some practice.

Example 1y:

Now repeat those examples and start on a middle finger pluck instead of a pick. As before, saying "finger, pick, finger, pick" as you play will really help you focus. You're programming in a motion, and that requires attention.

Example 1z:

The act of pre-placing the fingers on the strings means that it's easy to cut notes from ringing out when playing like this. This actually can be desirable, so that hybrid picking is something you'll reach for often.

If you want to sound a little more like Brett Garsed, Tom Quayle or Brent Mason, you'll want to avoid this deadening, and the only way to do this is to keep your fingers in the vicinity of the string without resting on them. This is a much harder technique to develop, but it's worth putting in the time if you want to develop this pick-like attack with your fingers.

Take some time with this mechanic until your hand starts to feel at home resting on the strings and alternating between pick and finger. When you're ready, move on to Chapter Two where we'll address some one finger string skipping mechanics.

Chapter Two – Single Finger String Skipping

Now you're happily integrating the middle finger into some simple adjacent string crossing ideas, it's time to get deeper into the world of string crossing by skipping a string between the pick and plucking finger.

However, instead of using the ring finger, we'll still be using the stronger middle finger. Mechanically, the only difference is that the hand must open up to create a larger gap between the pick and the middle finger. The middle, ring and pinkie fingers are still together, but there's now a gap between the pick and middle finger.

You can get used to this idea by working on the same pre-placement concept of Chapter One and practicing your hand positioning as follows. Begin by placing the pick on the D string, with the middle, ring and pinkie fingers on the G, B and high E strings respectively. Now, while keeping those fingers on the strings, move the pick over to the A string. Learning to feel comfortable with this gap between the pick and middle finger is an integral part of the hybrid picking technique, as you won't always be picking adjacent strings.

Now play Example 2a and alternate between picking on the A string and plucking with the middle finger on the G string.

Example 2a:

This idea can be applied anywhere. If the pick is on the D string, you should be comfortable plucking the B string with the middle finger.

Example 2b:

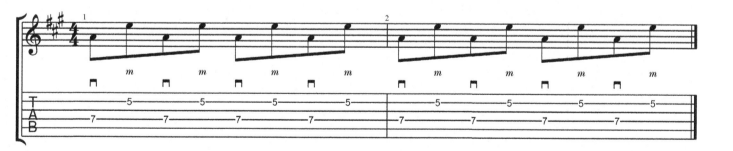

The following example takes a barred A major chord and alternates between the pick and middle finger while moving across each string set.

Remember, the movement between strings comes from the elbow, while the actual picking motion comes from the fingers. The wrist should be doing very little here.

Example 2c:

Here's that same idea, but now playing each grouping just once. This presents a further challenge as you need to change string groups more often.

Example 2d:

If you want to methodically apply these picking concepts, playing intervals is a great place to focus. 6ths in particular are useful because they sound cool (they have a definite Country edge) and they force you to mix adjacent and string crossing mechanics.

Here's a series of 6ths played across the neck using the notes of the A Mixolydian scale. If you're getting lost on the fingering here, use one finger per fret for the first measure then, as you move up the G and B strings, use the middle and ring fingers on the 7th fret. Then shift those fingers up to the 9th fret and back down.

Example 2e:

Next, here's a Country lick to try in A that features a series of descending 6ths from the Mixolydian mode and moves across the strings. Pay attention to the picking!

Example 2f:

Here's an idea that takes an octave and slides it up the G and E strings. Again, there are only downstrokes with the pick combined with middle finger plucks.

Example 2g:

In the shred world, guys like Greg Howe and Andy James are big fans of these string-skipped arpeggio patterns, and with hybrid picking at the ready, it becomes relatively easy to play them at speed.

Here's a string skipping pattern applied to a DMaj7 (D, F#, A, C#) arpeggio. Use the fretting hand index finger on the first note then, after hammering on to the 9th fret, move over to the G string with the index finger again, not the middle finger.

Example 2h:

Here's the same pattern applied to an F#m7 (F#, A, C#, E) arpeggio.

Licks like these may appear challenging at first, but remember that the reason you're working on hybrid picking is to reduce the amount of movement in your picking hand and develop a whole new level of fluency. Stick with it!

Example 2i:

Once you've developed some proficiency in alternating between downstrokes and plucking with the middle finger, it's time to introduce some pick up-strokes into the equation.

This is more challenging than just using downstrokes because the upward motion in the thumb and index finger makes it quite tricky to execute a solid pluck with the middle finger immediately after.

Let's isolate that mechanical movement so you can see what I mean. Play this example with an upstroke on the D string, then pluck the B string with the middle finger.

Example 2j:

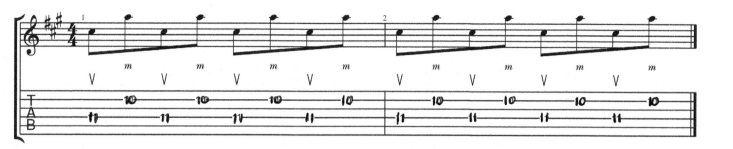

The following example shows a vintage Country guitar idea. It features three alternate picked notes on the G string, followed by a plucked note on the high E string. To make this lick to come alive, add some speed and palm mute the G string! One tip: don't try and barre over from the G to E string here. It's OK to use the ring finger for the final note on the G string, then the pinkie to fret the high E string.

Example 2k:

This may raise the question, "So, what happens when there are just *two notes* before a hybrid-picked note?" The answer is that we create the same tricky mechanic as Example 2j, where we pluck after an upstroke!

Example 2l:

While it's worth putting some time into trying to improve this particular mechanic, it's also worth noting that every puzzle has a solution. This example is much easier to play if you begin with an upstroke, so you'll play *up, down, pluck, up, down, pluck.*

This may feel odd at first, but I can assure you, it's one of the most useful hybrid picking movements you can master.

Example 2m:

Now here's that same mechanic applied in the middle of a Rock 'n' Roll blues riff. We'll bring this to life in a later chapter, but you need to get comfortable with this upstroke idea before you get there.

Example 2n:

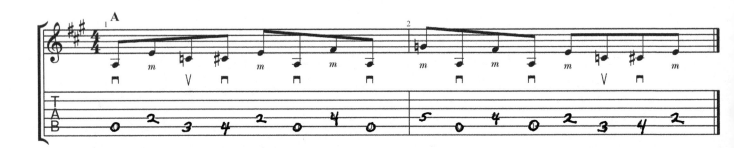

Now you've got a feel for skipping one string between the pick and fingers, it's time to stretch things out by anchoring the pick on the D string and moving the middle finger between the G, B and E strings, while holding down an A major triad.

Example 2o:

Here's a similar idea applied to a chord progression in the key of A. When you're comfortable with the hybrid picking, give this a go with just the pick and see how much work you're saving yourself!

Example 2p:

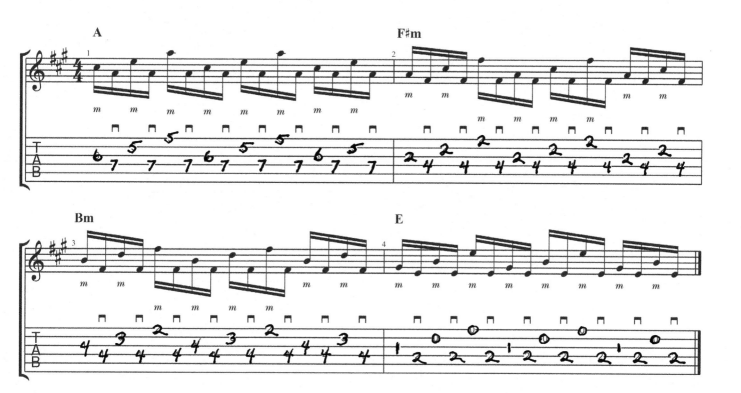

An excellent way to practice expanding and contracting the gap between pick and fingers is to keep the middle finger on one string and move the pick across different strings. Try this technique with an A major chord.

Example 2q:

Here's that idea with a longer chord progression and a bit more soul!

Example 2r:

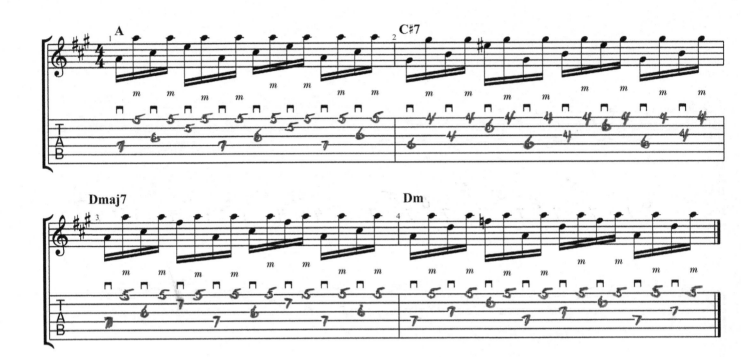

It's this same mechanic that Eric Johnson uses at the end of the intro to his classic song *Cliffs of Dover*. This lick turned heads when he played it back in the early '90s and it still holds up today!

Example 2s:

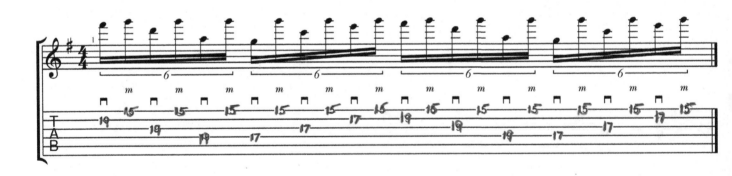

Licks like these are known as *pedal points* as they feature a repeating note. It's fun to explore ideas like playing an E at the 12th fret and descending an E Major scale underneath it. It's a nice little fingering challenge too. It's unlikely you'll play this in a solo, but it's certainly a nice technical workout.

Example 2t:

Growing up, Steve Morse was one of my guitar heroes. I loved the way he played in the Dixie Dregs, with rock chops to die for, but with elements of Classical, Country and Jazz thrown in. While he's a great hybrid picker, he's also one of the best players of fast alternate picked arpeggios. I could never get close to playing those patterns at speed, but I love applying some of these hybrid patterns to his chord progressions.

Although the hybrid motion between strings is adjacent, this example fits here because after hybrid picking the D string, we jump over to pick the B string.

Example 2u:

The final exercise of this chapter is inspired by Bluegrass and sounds a bit like a repeating banjo roll. The trick here is to drill the hybrid picking until it feels natural. Once you've got that little finger twister down, it should be pretty easy.

Example 2v:

Now you've got some of the fundamental techniques down, I wanted to write a short solo example that will allow you to practice these concepts in a more musical context.

This example takes place in a rockier setting, over a riff in G minor, with the notes coming almost entirely from the G Minor Pentatonic scale (G, Bb, C, D, F). The notes A and Db have been added for a little bit of colour.

You'll be using a combination of hybrid picking on adjacent strings and string skipping ideas, so pay careful attention to the picking directions.

The challenge here is that there are a lot of position shifts, as you take pattens and move them up and down the neck. Spend some time getting familiar with the notes you need to play before building up any speed.

Example 2w:

Right! You've made it through the alternate picking bootcamp. Take some time to get comfortable with these ideas and when ready, move on to the next chapter where we'll start looking the *pinch* technique.

Chapter Three – The Pinch Technique & Hybrid Picked Chords

Everything you've played so far has used an alternating hybrid picking motion and been played one note at a time. As explained earlier, all these examples *could,* in theory, have been played with a pick. Sure, they wouldn't sound quite the same and it would be considerably more work... but it's possible.

For me, however, the beauty of hybrid picking is using it to explore melodic ideas that you *can't play* with a pick, and one of the biggest benefits is applying it to chordal ideas. In this chapter you'll learn to play *harmonic* hybrid picking with more than one note played simultaneously. To execute these kinds of phrases you'll need to get to grips with the *pinch* technique.

As the name suggests, the idea is to use a pinching motion between the pick and fingers to play strings simultaneously. NB: You don't keep the fingers stiff or lift the wrist to do this.

Let's learn this approach with a simple double-stop.

Place the pick on the D string and rest the middle finger on the B string. Then, using a pinching motion, pluck both strings together. Your fingers should move into your hand, and your hand shouldn't move away from the strings.

Example 3a:

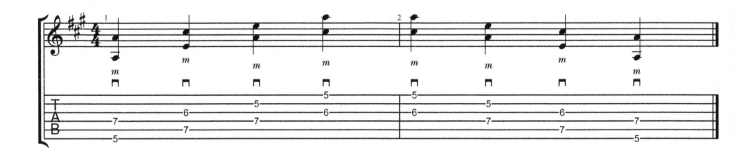

Here's the same idea but moving between string sets on a barred A major chord.

Example 3b:

To improve your fluency, let's return to the stretching patterns from the previous chapter and play them with the pinch technique. First, keep the middle finger on the high E string and move the pick between the D, G and B strings.

Example 3c:

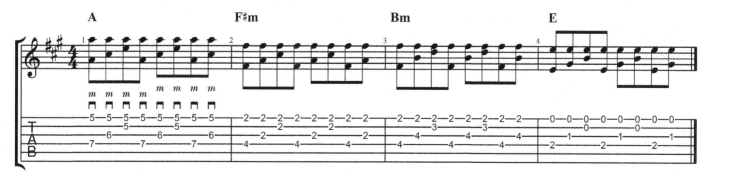

This time move the *plucking finger* across the strings. I decided to mix this one up a little with some Ted Greene style voicings.

Example 3d:

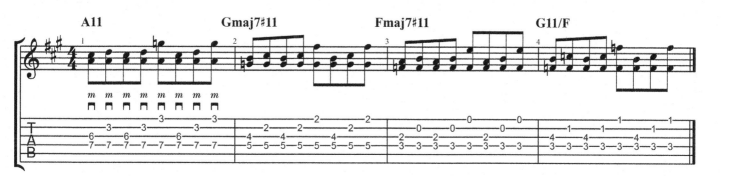

While you *could* strum these ideas with a pick, it would sound completely different. Hybrid picking makes you sound a lot more like a swing or stride piano player.

In this example, any time you have two notes on the same fret, don't use a barre, instead use the ring and pinkie fingers to fret each note.

Example 3e:

This pinching motion isn't limited to wider intervals like 6ths. In fact, a big part of my playing style is using this motion to strike adjacent strings without creating a strum sound. Let's apply this idea to an A major chord. Hold down the full chord down and sound each note with the pick and a finger.

Example 3f:

A great way to make this idea musical is to use the chord pattern but slide into each double-stop from a semitone below. This puts you in instant pedal steel territory but also summons up the playing of the incredible Jim Campilongo or Jimmy Bryant.

Example 3g:

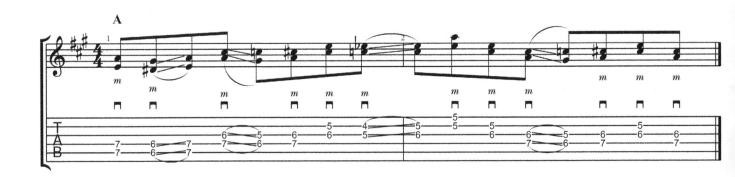

Here's another one of these little double-stop ideas, moving from an open A chord up to the 5th fret area. I think of these things as Scotty Anderson licks for humans who can't play as fast as Scotty.

Example 3h:

Here's a slightly trickier line in the same vein, which takes you from the 6th fret all the way up to the 12th.

In both measures here you'll find double stops that use the same fingering. When playing them, use the ring and index finger, and shift the hand up chromatically between chords.

Example 3i:

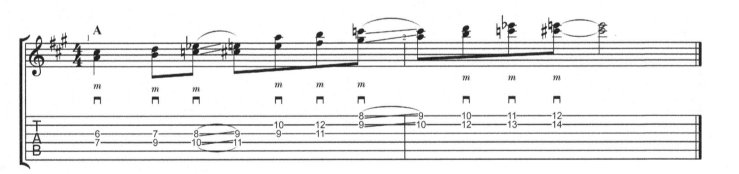

Another common application of hybrid picked chords is to play in 10ths. A 10th is simply a 3rd played an octave higher and is found easily in the common E Major shape barre chord.

The following example shows full C and G chords, then the 10th intervals are isolated. Play them with a pick and middle finger pinch.

Example 3j:

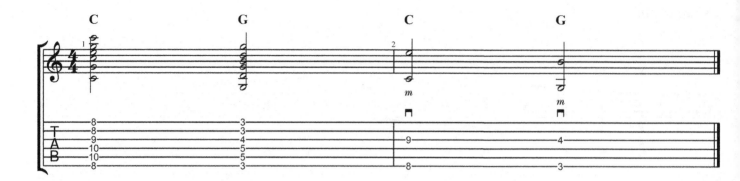

These types of voicings are used in everything from Jazz (our own Martin Taylor is a big fan!) to Pop, as this example similar to The Red Hot Chilli Peppers' *Scar Tissue* shows.

In this example you need to combine both the alternating hybrid motion and the pinch.

Example 3k:

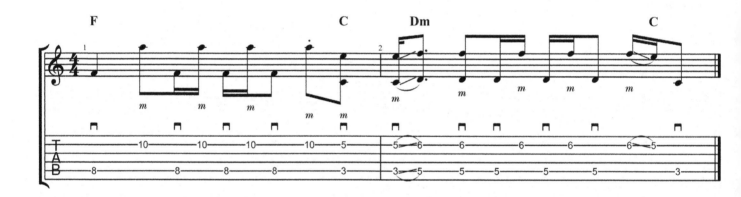

The following example of hybrid picked 10ths is reminiscent of a System of a Down B-side!

While ideas like this could be played fingerstyle, having the dexterity to hybrid pick them will mean you can integrate them into your playing without finding a way to drop your pick and grab it again when you need it.

Example 3l:

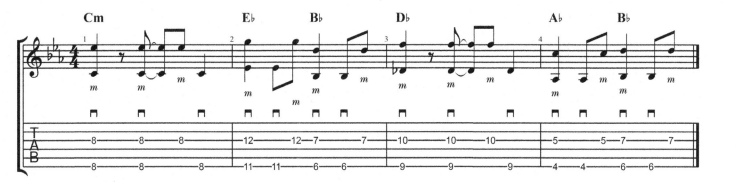

Here's something a bit more bluesy, inspired by the great boogie woogie piano players. And, it's almost impossible to execute with a pick alone! This is a wonderful lick to throw in when playing over an E Major or E7 chord in any setting.

Example 3m:

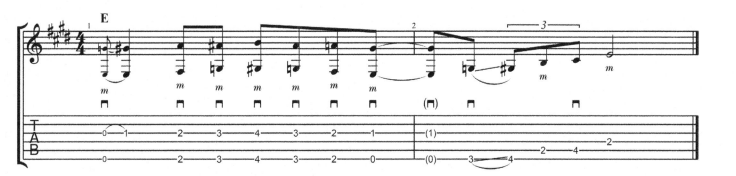

Let's look at some cool blues rhythm guitar ideas that use the middle finger to spice things up.

First up, alternate between pinches on the A and G strings, and palm muted open E bass notes. Each bass note is played with a picked downstroke but pinch the plucked notes on the beats.

Example 3n:

Now let's flesh that idea out by adding a little more interest and moving from an E major to an A major.

Example 30:

This final example is an introduction to the wonderful world of Travis picking and a teaser for something coming later in the book.

This is a simple rendition of the start of the classic Folk tune, *Camptown Races*. Use the pick to play the bass notes on every beat, and the middle finger to pick out the melody on the top three strings.

Example 3p:

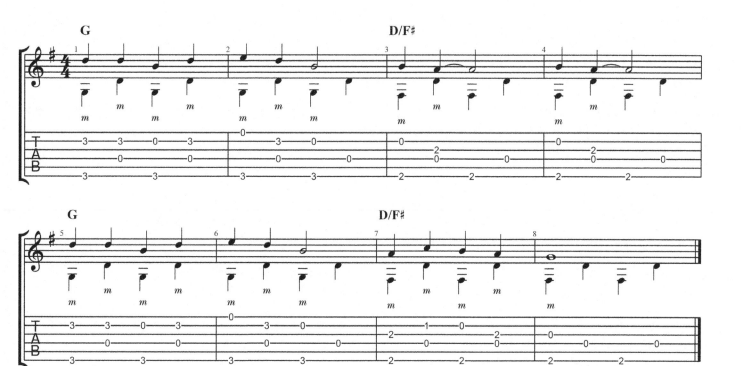

By now, you should have developed a reasonable degree of dexterity in your picking and be able play licks that require you to alternate between the pick and the finger. You've also learned some nice chordal ideas.

As you can see, we're just getting into the material and we're still only getting warmed up.

Hopefully you're starting to see how efficient just the middle finger can be when playing licks and chords. So why not start unlocking our real potential by adding another finger into the equation?

Get practicing and I'll see you in the next chapter!

Chapter Four – Adding the Ring Finger

The real magic of hybrid picking starts to open up when you introduce a second finger to the party. There are a variety of ways you're able to use those other fingers in different musical settings, but in this chapter, you'll be limited to using the middle and ring fingers as one unit for playing double-stops. This will allow you time to develop the necessary mechanics and dexterity before working on finger independence.

It's unlikely you'll use this two-finger double-stop approach to play high distortion Metal, but for Country, Blues and Rock players, it's often the bread and butter of their sound. You'll struggle to find any hot playing from guys like Josh Smith, Albert Lee or Johnny Hiland, where this isn't one of the key ingredients of their sound. There are some exciting possibilities here – and it's nowhere near as complicated as you might initially think.

You'll recall that the focus of Chapter One was the pre-placement of the fingers. We used that approach to get a feel for the correct/most comfortable posture, but now you'll use it to play some outrageously cool licks!

To get started, we'll use a simple A major triad on the D, G and B strings. Place the pick on the D string and the middle and ring fingers on the G and B respectively.

Begin by striking the D string with the pick, then pluck the G and B strings simultaneously using middle and ring fingers. I'll say it again, this doesn't happen by lifting the hand or twisting the wrist. The motion comes just from the fingers themselves.

Example 4a:

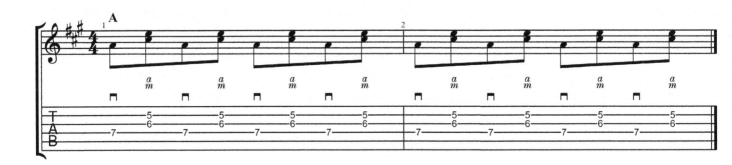

Here's a similar idea, but this time beginning with the pluck from the fingers. It's important you feel as comfortable plucking on the beat with the fingers as you do with the pick, and this kind of exercise will quickly build that independence.

Example 4b:

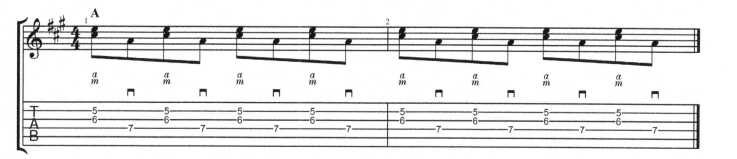

As before, you should practice these mechanics on different string groupings. Here's the same idea applied to the A, D and G strings. When this feels comfortable, try moving it to any three-string grouping.

Example 4c:

Now let's add a gap between the pick and fingers like before, as this will often be required. The following example picks the D string and plucks the B and E.

Example 4d:

Now you have the basic idea down, let's explore some more musical applications by introducing a bit of movement in the fretting hand.

This idea features alternating double-stops between the C# and E, and D and F#. In order to play the second double-stop, roll over with the ring finger of the left hand, playing the 7th fret with a barred finger.

Example 4e:

A common trick in this position is to hold the index finger in a mini-barre at the 5th fret to play the G and B strings, then hammer on to the 6th fret of the G string – a classic bluesy minor to major 3rd.

Example 4f:

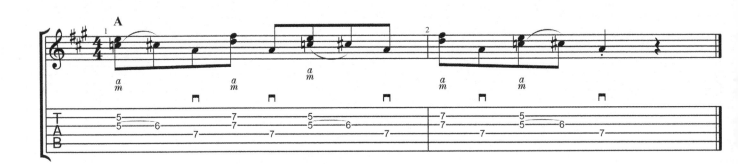

Another slight twist is to slide into the A chord from a semitone below. This takes the lick from the Blues to more of a Country sound.

Example 4g:

In the next example we add another double-stop on the 5th fret of the B and E strings. You'll need to cross over a set of strings with the picking hand fingers, so take your time and build up speed gradually.

Example 4h:

Taking a step away from the Country vibe, here's an open A position blues riff. This forces you to practice the same motion on a different set of strings. Remember to move over strings from the elbow, not the wrist.

Example 4i:

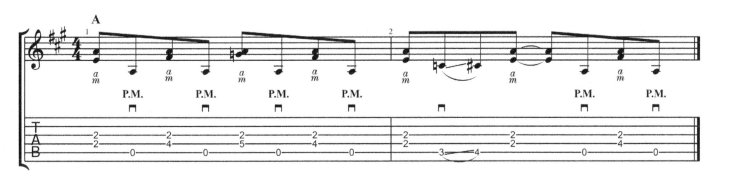

A great idea used by Jerry Reed and Brent Mason involves using these double-stops in the open position, keeping the top note static while the bottom note descends chromatically. This is a bit of a finger twister, but it sounds great and is well worth the effort.

Play the first double-stop with the index finger, then move the index finger down while fretting the 2nd fret G string with the middle finger. This sets you up to do the slide on the A string with the ring finger.

Example 4j:

Now you're starting to get to grips with this two-finger motion, here's another finger twister around the E shape of an A major chord voicing. Shifting between positions and string sets should keep you on your toes.

Example 4k:

This line descends from the 5th fret to an open position A major chord. These types of lines can inspire unlimited musical options, so spend time exploring this movement.

Example 4l:

Now we move into Brent Mason territory with an up-tempo double-stop lick. The trick here is playing two consecutive hybrid picked notes towards the end of the second bar. It requires some speed in the picking hand fingers to avoid alternating between the pick and the fingers, so build up the speed over time.

Example 4m:

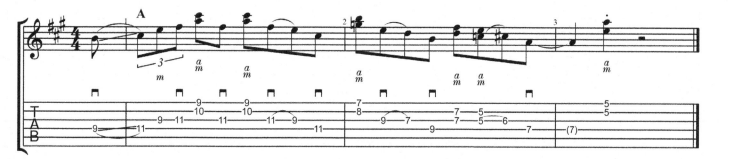

If you're having problems with the speed required in the previous example, isolate the idea and work on it. Becoming fluent with your technique will often require being able to diagnose your personal challenges and figure out the solution. This book will be able to take you most of the way, but developing a sense of exploration based on what you discover here is important too.

The following example requires you to play consecutive double-stops with the picking hand fingers. This will require some practice as the fingers are pre-placed for the first of the double-stops, but then need to come back in and pluck the strings from nowhere immediately after this. Take this slowly and gradually bring it up to tempo.

Example 4n:

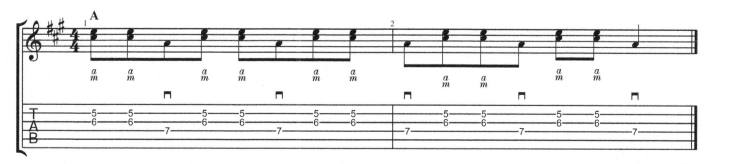

Here's the same double plucked idea from the last example applied to a repeating figure.

Example 4o:

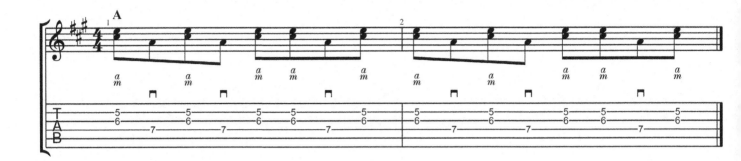

Moving back down to the open position, here's a groove that uses both the upstroke technique combined with consecutive double-stops in the picking hand fingers.

Example 4p:

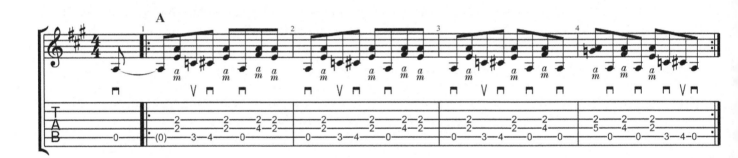

If you're struggling with a particular mechanic, the best thing to do is to work on it in isolation, to maximise the efficiency of your practice time. For example, the up-stroke technique is a lot of fun to work on at speed with triplets.

Pluck *up, down, pluck, up, down* in the next example.

Example 4q:

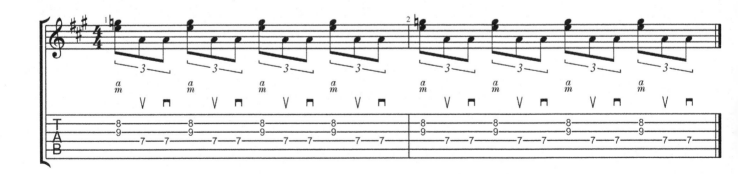

When played in the middle of a phrase that's not played in a triplet rhythm, you can come up with some wild rhythmic patterns.

In order to make the lick as simple as possible, focus on barring the 7th fret double-stop with the ring finger. This sets you up for the position change much more effectively.

Example 4r:

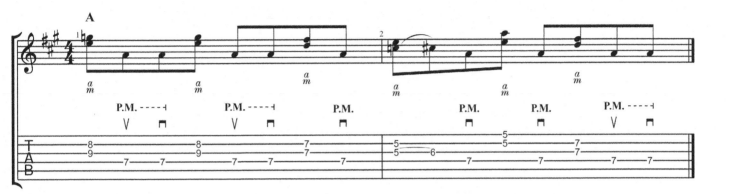

Here's a slightly more extreme example in the style of Country shred maestro, Johnny Hiland. You'll cover a huge range of the neck here, so be careful with those position shifts.

Example 4s:

All these examples have alternated between the pick and the fingers, but it's also possible to apply the pinching technique to play three notes simultaneously. Let's begin by playing a three-note pinch with the pick, middle and ring fingers.

Example 4t:

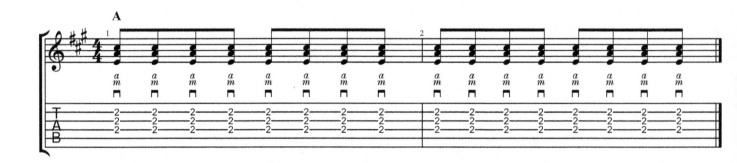

Here's that pinching motion applied to four three-string groupings of an E major chord. This forces you to get comfortable changing strings while keeping your picking hand pre-placement position under control.

Example 4u:

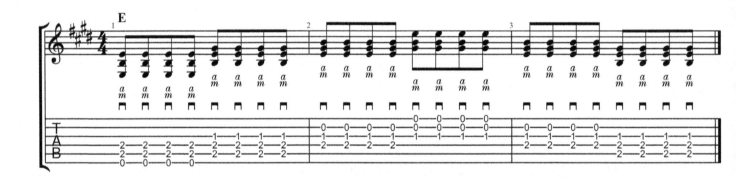

Once you've got this idea down it becomes quite easy to apply it to chordal riffs like this Blues Rock idea in A. You'll be using the pick on every note and pinching with the pick and fingers for the chord stabs.

Example 4v:

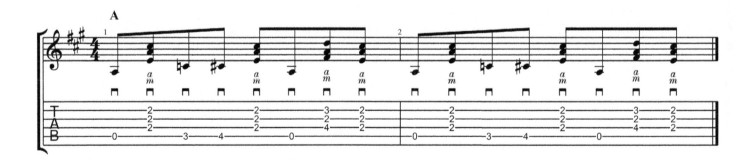

This Gospel type riff reminds me of Robben Ford's early Yellowjackets playing. Keep a palm mute on the notes on the low E string and let all the chords ring out.

Example 4w:

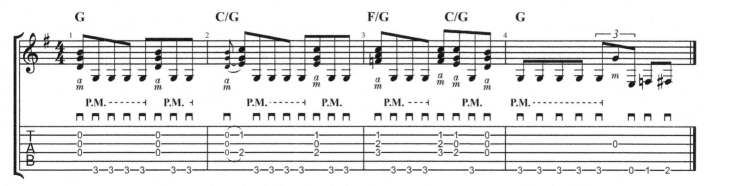

The next idea is a Hammond organ style lick. As with the previous idea, you'll use the pick for all the notes on the A string *and* each of the triple-stop chord voicings.

The only tricky part here is the triplet at the beginning of the second bar. Reach out for the note on the high E string with your middle finger as you have done in previous chapters.

Example 4x:

The final example is a longer, more musical idea that you'll really be able to get your teeth into. This was developed from one of the pieces in my *100 Licks for Country Guitar* book and showcases how you can use double-stops in an up-tempo Country Rock type setting.

The only part that may give you some bother is the repeating motif in the first measure, but apply the same fingering you used for Example 4j and you'll be fine.

Example 4y:

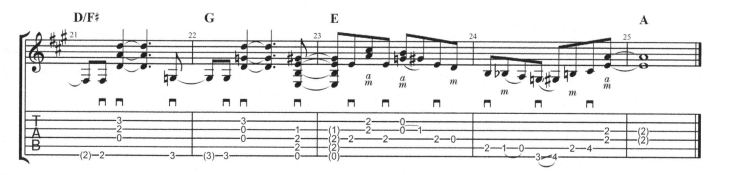

It would be easy to fill a whole book with licks just like this, and that's before we've begun to apply these approaches to riffs and songs. However, we need to move on, so I encourage you to see how you can apply these techniques to songs or riffs you already know. Get creative and see how the new ideas can push your playing a new direction.

When you're comfortable with these ideas, move forward and we'll start developing even more independence between your fingers to build more advanced, intricate *rolling* techniques.

See you there!

Chapter Five – Finger Independence

While the discipline required to develop proper classical fingerstyle technique (and nail maintenance!) isn't for me, I've still always had tremendous respect for the jaw-dropping music of Sor, Segovia and Giuliani. These musicians led me to Flamenco players like Paco De Lucia, and new worlds of technical proficiency explored in Russian Classical guitar and Brazilian Choro players.

Playing their ideas with a pick was impossible, so my arpeggio technique was largely limited to sweep picking *a la* Yngwie Malmsteen and Jason Becker.

When I was 17, however, *Total Guitar* magazine published a video lesson with Australian guitarist Brett Garsed and suddenly everything changed for me. Brett played with a pick, but used his middle, ring and even pinkie finger to execute arpeggios with blistering speed and precision.

I spent a lot of time working on this approach and now my middle and ring fingers feel just as effective as my pick. This was, in no small part, due to also discovering the phenomenal playing of Danny Gatton, and some of his long out of circulation videos. This level of technique is something you can achieve, it's just a matter of working on the right exercises for long enough.

In this chapter, I'll show you the exercises that will quickly boost your hybrid picking independence and fluency. As before, everything begins with pre-placement.

In the next example, place the pick on the D string, with the middle and ring fingers resting on the G and B strings respectively.

Pick the D string then, beginning the motion from the fingers, pluck the G and B strings consecutively. This is called a forward roll. Work with a metronome, start slowly, and gradually speed this up.

Example 5a:

The previous example featured an A major triad played with a triplet rhythm and the picked note always fell nicely on the down beat. While this is a nice way to begin working on your independence, to improve your technique we really need to give you some more rhythmic challenges.

A great way to work on this is by offsetting the finger that starts the pattern. Instead of beginning with the pick, play the same sequence but starting with the note under the middle finger. Again, start slow and gradually speed up with a metronome. The goal is to play with a nice even dynamic. The picked note shouldn't be any louder than the plucked notes.

Example 5b:

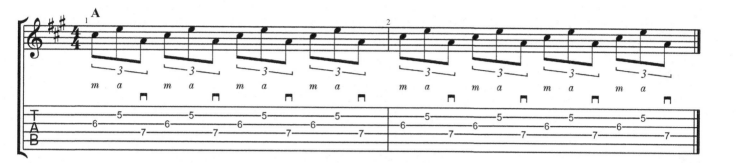

Now begin on the ring finger and repeat the process.

Example 5c:

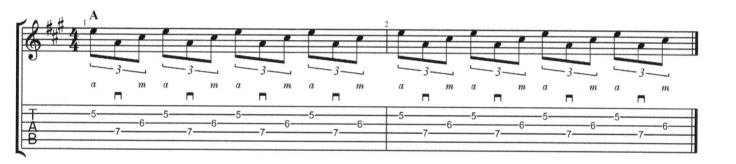

Now we'll apply this approach to a 1/16th note rhythm. As you're playing four notes per click in groups of three, it means that the picked note moves a 1/16th note backwards every cycle and you're having to pick the downbeat with a different digit each time.

This can be practiced in two ways. The first is to accent the picked notes (the bold numbers):

1 2 3 **1** 2 3 **1** 2 3 **1** 2 3

Example 5d:

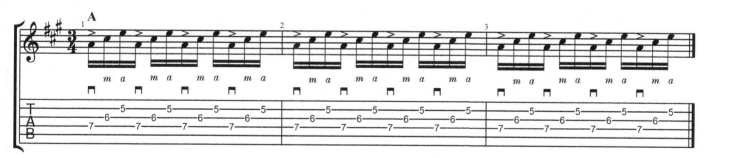

Or, to accent the notes that fall on the beats:

1 2 3 **1** 2 3 **1** 2 3 **1** 2 3

Pay careful to the audio and compare both examples. Learning both these inflections with confidence is an important part of developing control in your picking hand.

Example 5e:

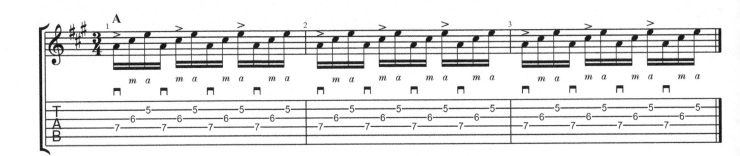

To begin developing some real speed, I want you to apply the *Spanish laps* approach. Imagine jogging the length of a football field and then sprinting its width. In other words, you practice the pattern slowly, then push for some severe short bursts of speed. Applied to the forward roll we've been learning, you should play the 1/16th note pattern three times, followed by two 1/16th note triplet groups.

Example 5f:

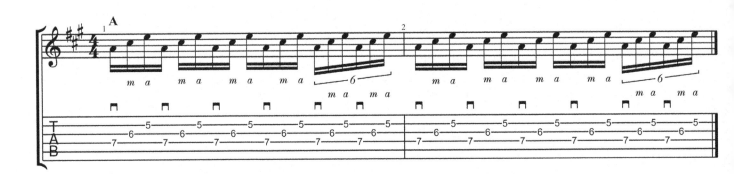

Apply this same approach to the string change arpeggio ideas. First try it on the A, D and G string group, then the D, G and B strings.

Your wrist position shouldn't change too much here. Any tiny movement comes from the elbow, moving the hand across the strings, so your pre-placement position still feels the same.

Example 5g:

This idea can be expanded by crossing all three-string groups to practice the feeling of moving across strings.

Example 5h:

Here's an idea that combines a two-string motif with a repeating three-string motif. You'll execute this using first the pick, then middle finger, before moving the pick over to the G string and playing a forward roll.

This is a nice solution to the technical problem of ascending through five strings without enough fingers! You'll be using this pattern extensively later in the book when working on some Bach, so pay attention now.

Example 5i:

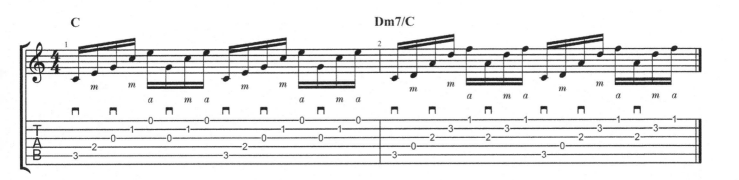

Moving forward rolls between adjacent string sets is a common idea. In the next example, begin on the E string, play a forward roll, then move to the A string and repeat the idea across this E Major chord.

Example 5j:

The next example is a little more challenging and is built around playing a six-note ascending arpeggio. Play a forward roll starting on the E string, then another starting on the G. This movement requires a high degree of control in your picking hand as you're having to jump over multiple string sets.

Example 5k:

Here's the same ascending arpeggio, but now played with the Spanish lap approach to help you build some speed with the transition.

Example 5l:

Now let's look at some licks that use the forward roll concept.

First up is a slippery little lick over a G chord with some jazzy chromaticism. There are a lot of open strings in this lick, which sound a bit cooler if you let them all ring out. The second part of the lick uses some basic double-stops ideas.

Example 5m:

This example falls somewhere between a riff and a lick and is definitely the type of thing you could throw in when riffing around an open A chord! Spent some time working on the slides in the second bar.

Example 5n:

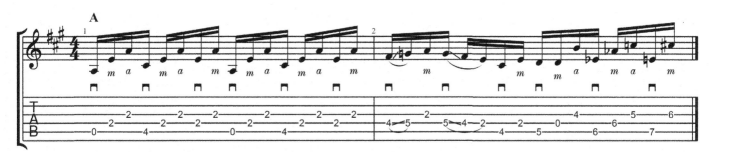

This Blues Rock idea combines some forward rolls with alternating between the pick and middle finger.

Example 5o:

The opposite of the forward roll is the *reverse roll*. These feel a little less comfortable to play than the forward roll and are worth exploring to build your independence and fluency.

This A major triad descends from the highest note. Start with the ring finger, then the middle, then the pick.

Example 5p:

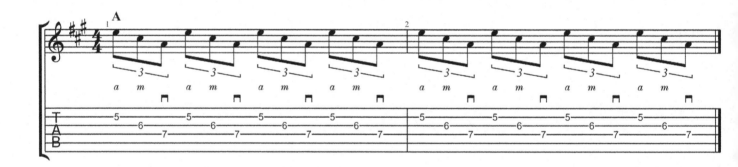

The best way to develop fluency with this motion is to cycle the digit that begins the pattern, as before. Here's that idea with the middle finger first.

Example 5q:

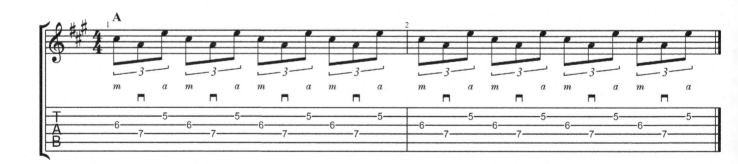

And now the pick.

Example 5r:

Let's apply the Spanish lap concept to the reverse roll. Start at a reasonable pace and gradually increase the speed when your fingers get comfortable with the movement.

Example 5s:

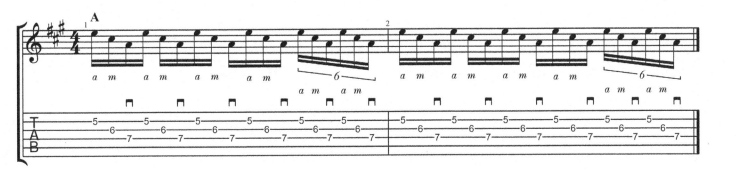

Again, this exercise can be made more challenging by cycling the starting note. Here's the same idea, but now starting on the middle finger.

Example 5t:

And once again, starting on the pick.

Example 5u:

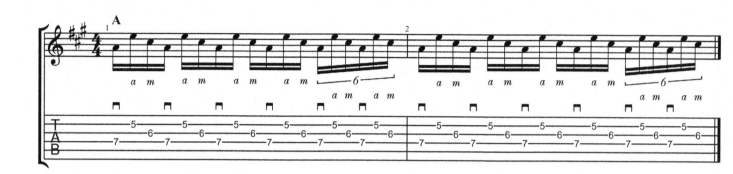

When you're comfortable with this reverse roll motion, it makes sense to begin working it across string sets. Learn this idea and shoot for accuracy before speed.

Example 5v:

Now let's look at some musical applications that will get your creative juices flowing.

First up is a Jerry Reed inspired lick with a cool open string idea in the first bar. It contains ascending and descending open string scale runs in the second bar too. Let the strings ring out as much as possible.

Example 5w:

Here's an idea inspired by Albert Lee. It begins with a tricky descent, followed by a straightforward run up the A Major Pentatonic scale.

Example 5x:

Now you've covered the forward and reverse rolls, it's time to combine them into one smooth up and down motion.

Begin with a pick, ascend through the shape, then pluck the G string again on the way down before repeating.

You'll find that you can't pre-place a finger on the descent, as it's just left the G string when ascending. This results in something more akin to a floating hand, so it might feel a little awkward at first.

Example 5y:

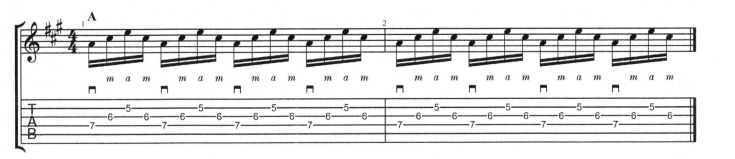

The next example is a handy mechanic to develop because it allows you to change the direction of your arpeggio patterns, mid run.

Example 5z:

Here's one final arpeggio pattern that ascends and descends in position. The focus here isn't on the music, it's about developing a high level of dexterity so that later you can play whatever you want.

Example 5z1:

These multi-finger techniques need to ferment in your playing over a period of weeks, months and years. The goal here to develop enough dexterity that you can play anything without thinking. Don't worry if it takes time to develop though – when it clicks, you'll have built a playing style that's incredibly powerful and unique to you. It's worth the effort.

I wanted to end this chapter with something a little longer and more musical, so I've composed a little etude over a 12-bar blues that will allow you to get some of these techniques together.

There's nothing out of the ordinary here, but the transitions between riff and ascending/descending licks might feel a little jarring. Make you're 100% confident with the notes you have to play, and the technique needed to play them, so when you play them at speed it's effortless.

Example 5z2:

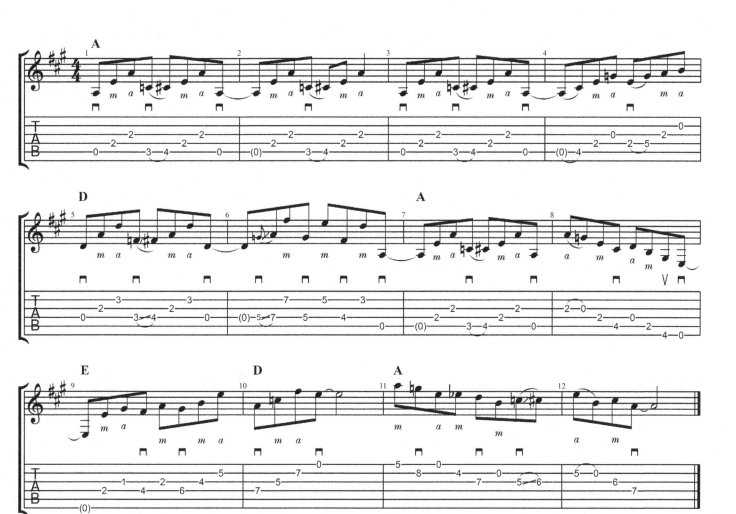

In the next chapter, we're going to develop some power and control in the guitar picker's nemesis – the pinkie finger!

Chapter Six – Three-Finger Chord Development

There's no hiding from the fact that, for most of us, the pinkie finger is pretty uncoordinated compared to the other fingers. There are biological reasons for this and there's a lot of talk about flexor tendons and other factors way above my paygrade, but essentially, the ring finger and pinkie tend to work in tandem as they share many components in the hand.

Another issue with the pinkie finger is that it's significantly shorter than the ring finger, meaning you need to contort your fingers in a way they don't naturally fall to place the tips of the ring and pinkie fingers on the strings at the same time.

That doesn't mean it isn't possible though. In fact, for simple plucked chords it's relatively easy.

If you look back to the start of this book, the first exercise had you placing the pick on one string and pre-placing the middle, ring and pinkie fingers on the three adjacent strings. If you do that now, you should be able to pinch with the pick and the three fingers to sound all four notes simultaneously.

Example 6a:

Try applying that motion to the top four strings while holding down an E major chord.

Example 6b:

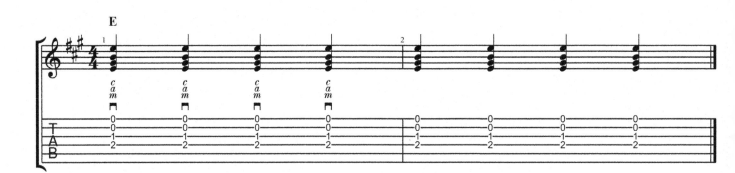

Next, try the same motion with a one-string gap between the pick and fingers. This is another position for chordal playing.

Example 6c:

Here's the same idea applied to a C#m7 chord, on the A, G, B and E strings.

Example 6d:

These two positions form about 95% of how this technique is used, so if you have these down then you've mastered the basic position.

Here's a jazzy blues that uses these two picking patterns. It certainly offers a different musical texture than strumming.

Example 6e:

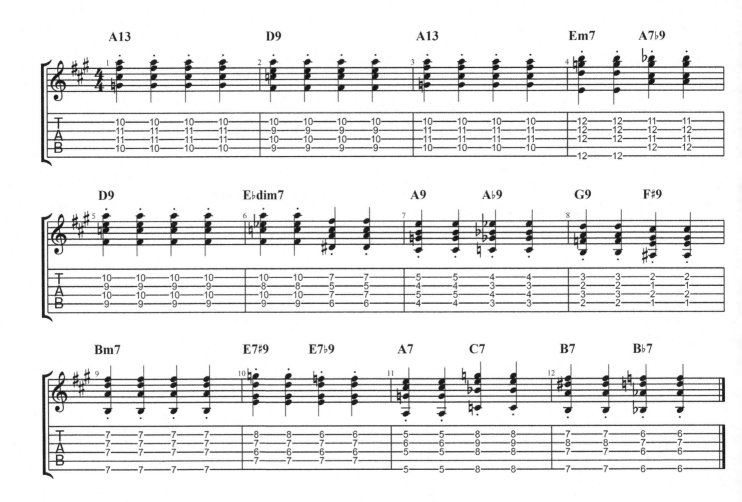

Once you've got a feel for pinching chords, it's time to start alternating between the pick and fingers. Here's one way to alternate the pick and fingers on an AMaj7 chord.

Example 6f:

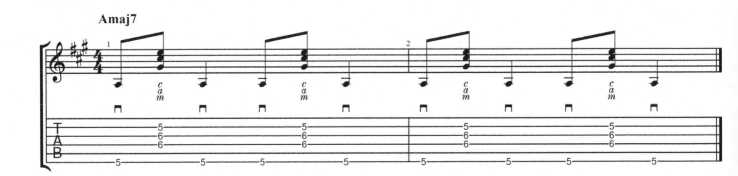

As you develop more proficiency with this technique, you'll quickly realise there's potential for almost limitless variation. Here's a short pattern that combines both pinched chords and alternating.

Example 6g:

Now try this simple Bossa Nova rhythm on the same AMaj7 chord. Take this rhythmic pattern and apply it to other chords and progressions that you know.

Example 6h:

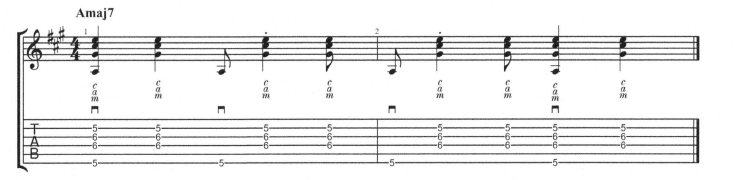

Here's a Cmaj9 chord with the root on the A string. Use the first finger of your fretting hand to alternate between the A and E strings to create an authentic bass movement.

Example 6i:

The next example is almost identical to the last but adds one more picked note on beat 2 before changing strings. This helps the Bosa Nova pattern sound a bit more authentic.

Example 6j:

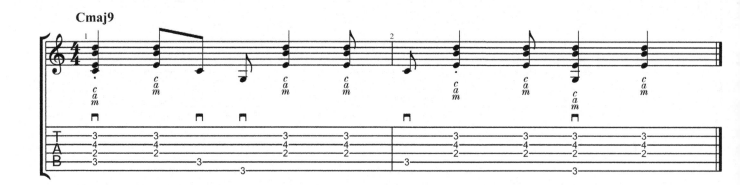

Now you've tried this picking motion, let's use it on a longer chord progression. This ii-V-I progression is one of the most common chord movements and here I've fleshed out those chords to the exotic sounding Dm9, G7#5 and C6/9 that you'd expect to hear in a bossa nova setting.

Example 6k:

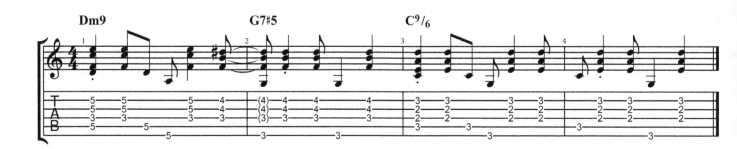

There is a world of Latin rhythms at your disposal, all of which lend themselves wonderfully to the hybrid picking technique. Check out this cool Samba pattern.

Example 6l:

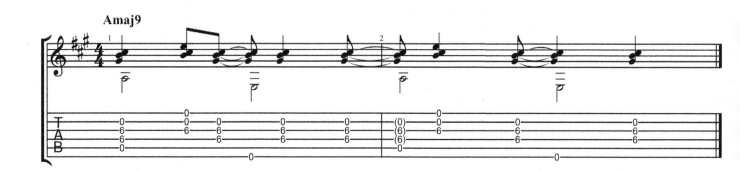

Another exciting way to use this hybrid approach is to help distinguish between walking basslines and chord stabs. The following example outlines the first part of a blues.

Begin by pinching the A7 chord with pick and fingers, then play the remaining bass notes with the pick before moving to the D9 chord for another pinch, and so on.

Example 6m:

This idea starts to sound more musical when you offset the chords, so they occur between the bass notes. The pattern is *pick, fingers, pick, pick, pick.*

Example 6n:

A fun way to work on this technique is to play a swung 1/8th note rhythm with alternate picking on the low string, then add chord stabs over the top with fingers. This helps you develop more independence between the pick and fingers.

Example 6o:

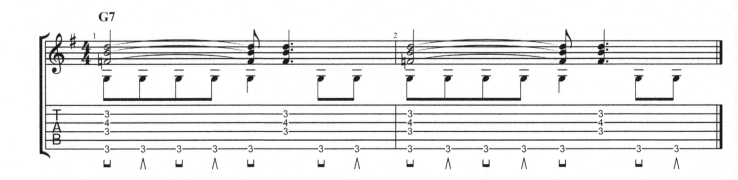

The next example is similar to last, except I've added an additional bass note. The extra note occurs on the same beat as the plucked chord and you'll need to play it with a pick upstroke. This is tricky, but not impossible. It may seem a lot of work for minimal payoff, because if you examine the audio for both examples, they both have the same vibe, but it's included here for the technical challenge.

Example 6p:

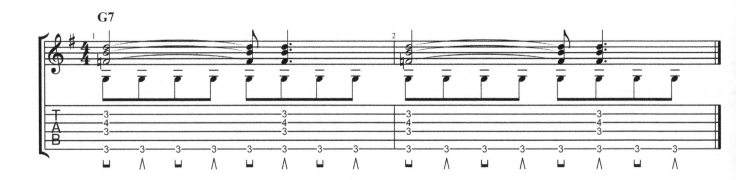

Here's a slightly more involved version of that last idea that alternates between two different chord voicings. There are two options for fingering this. You can either barre across the 3rd fret with the index finger and execute the hammer-on with the middle finger, playing the 5th fret with the ring finger, or play the chord like you did in the previous example, but use the thumb to fret the low E. Some might consider that a little more unconventional, but that's how I play it (and how players like Danny Gatton would do it).

Example 6q:

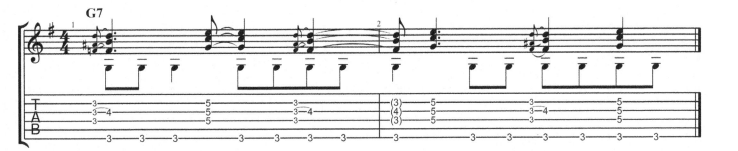

You can expand the previous idea by adding another G7 chord voicing on the top three strings. The challenge here is to master the accuracy of moving the three picking fingers from the middle strings to the top three. This is a great example of what fretting the low E string with the thumb can help facilitate. It can be done without, but the thumb makes it quite easy!

Example 6r:

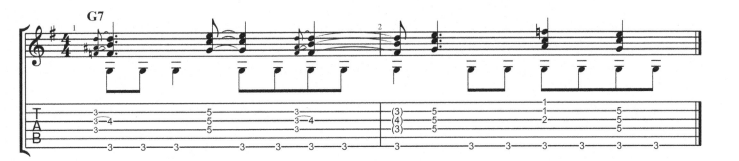

Let's expand the previous example with a few more chord voicings to keep improving your coordination. This has a Danny Gatton-meets-Gospel vibe and might inspire your own explorations of this sound.

You're still using the pick to play the bass note, but now you're mixing in various triads on top: G, C and F. The chord is still G7, you're just adding some colour.

Example 6s:

Here's the same kind of idea fleshed out to a full blues in G. There's nothing new happening here, just the same pattern from before moved up and down the neck to play each chord. However, building the stamina to play longer pieces is very important. Try applying these techniques to any songs that you know and see how long you can keep jamming for.

Example 6t:

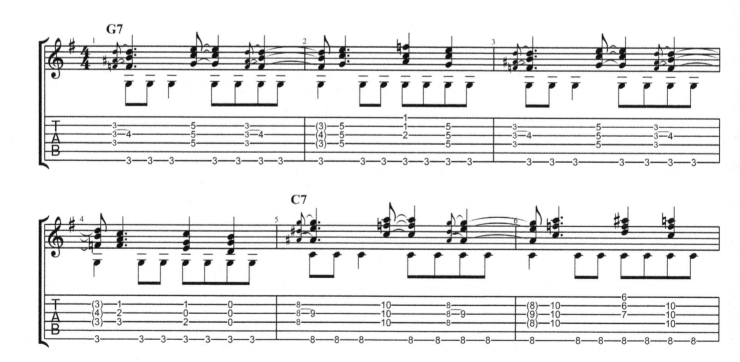

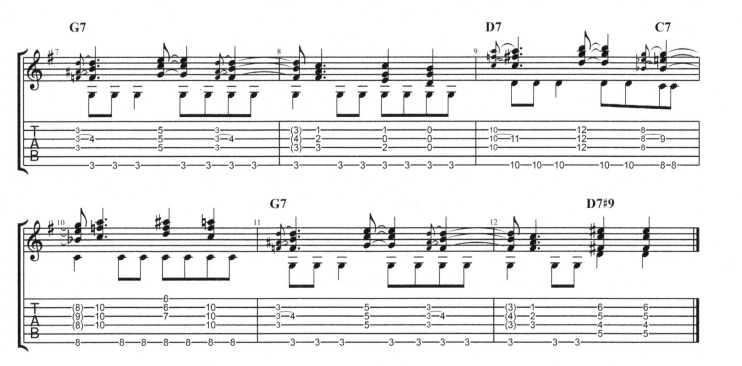

I want to finish this chapter by offering you a couple of ideas that use all three of your picking hand fingers to arpeggiate chords.

Let's begin by holding the AMaj7 chord with the pick and fingers pre-placed, then applying a full roll through each note in 1/8th notes.

Example 6u:

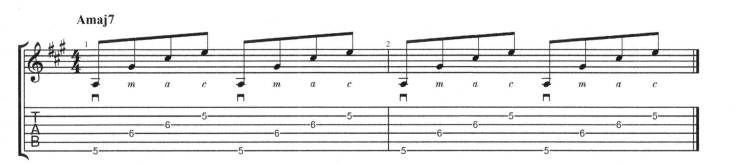

Here are same notes but with the rhythms mixed up and a triplet added to help you get a feel for accelerating during a phrase.

Example 6v:

Finally, let's speed up that motion so it feels like one smooth movement rather than four individual ones. The arpeggios are marked with wavy lines in the notation.

Example 6w:

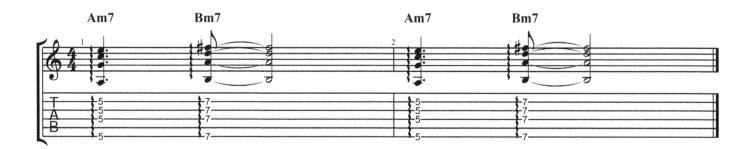

We'll be using the techniques covered in the chapter in the final piece, Break of the Dawn, later in the book. In the next chapter we'll be looking at some more advanced ideas to really get your fingers moving.

Chapter Seven – Advanced Finger Patterns

While the techniques covered so far will cater for 90% of your hybrid picking applications, there are some slightly more advanced and creative ways you can apply the technique. First let's look at how to play hybrid-picked open voiced triads in the style of Eric Johnson or Kiko Loureiro.

A *closed* voiced triad contains all three notes of a triad within an octave. The notes are on adjacent strings and played in order, so they're fairly easy to pick.

However, *open* voiced triads are created by shifting one of the notes in the triad up an octave. For example, you might take a C triad (C, E, G) then shift the note E up an octave (C, G, E). Open voiced triads always include at least one skipped string.

Listen to the difference between an open and closed voiced triad.

Example 7a:

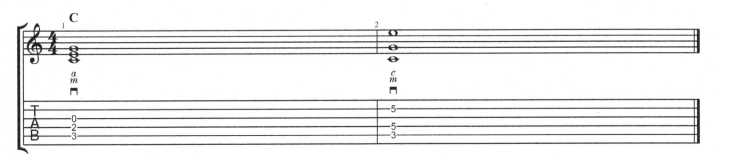

The open voiced triad creates an interesting technical challenge as there's a gap between the D and B string and the G string is not picked.

You might think that the best way to play this is to use the pick, middle and ring finger. This seems logical, but in fact, adds unnecessary complexity to your technique. In fact, the best way is to use the pick, middle and pinkie finger. As discussed earlier, creating a gap between the pick and fingers feels very easy, but trying to split those fingers up so they're not on adjacent strings is much harder.

To work on this, you again need to learn to pre-place you pick and fingers. The challenge is placing the middle and pinkie while leaving the ring finger out of the action. To do this, only pre-place the fingers you're using, so don't place the ring finger on the G string at all.

Try this technique with an open voiced C major triad that switches between inversions, first on the middle strings, then on the top strings.

Focus on the movement from placing the pick on the A string (and playing the A, D and B strings) to placing the pick on the D string (playing the D, G and E strings).

Example 7b:

Now try moving the triad down an inversion. To do this, you're going to skip the string adjacent to the pick. This time use the pick, middle and ring finger, as the gap between the pick and middle finger feels more natural.

Example 7c:

When you feel sufficiently comfortable with these two pick/finger movements, practice Example 7d – a selection of C major triad inversions that move from the 3rd fret, all the way up to the 15th.

Example 7d:

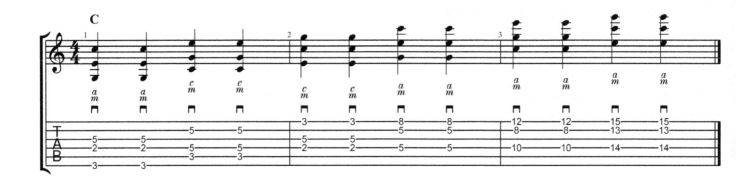

Another open voiced placement you'll need to master is a five-string pattern with a gap between each string. In this instance use the middle and pinkie for the higher two notes. Here's that placement applied to a C major chord. To train your muscle memory, place this exercise several times, each time completely removing both hands from the guitar.

Example 7e:

This new pick/finger placement is used in the following example that moves through different inversions of a C major chord. Take your time and learn this carefully – it's not easy! However, it's important to tackle more technically difficult exercises like this to improve your finger independence and dexterity.

Example 7f:

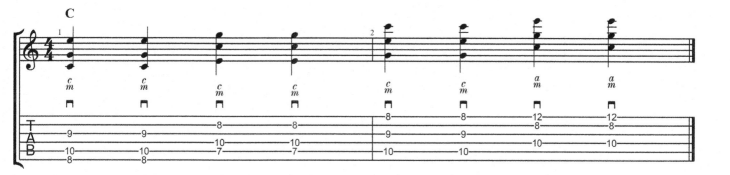

Here's an example of open voiced triads getting moved across multiple chord changes. If you add some chorus and delay, you'll quickly get into Eric Johnson territory.

Example 7g:

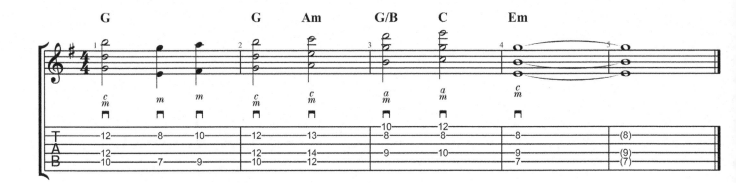

Here's another *trademark* Eric Johnson style lick, which combines open voiced triads with more traditional adjacent string triads. Here, you'll be mixing different string groupings, so pay careful attention to the picking notation so you don't get tripped up. The second half of the example moves you from open voiced triads to smaller three-string groupings.

Example 7h:

The following rhythm guitar part in B Minor would work wonderfully on a ballad. The hybrid picking adds a level of delicacy that's hard to replicate with the pick. Learn this sequence, then try playing it in other keys.

Example 7i:

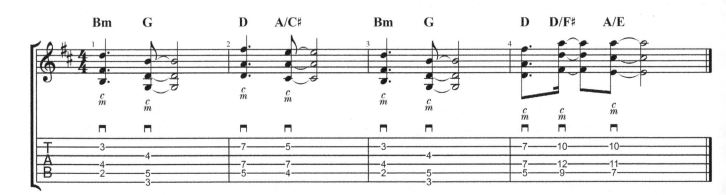

Now, here's a real challenge! In the next example, we'll play these open voiced triad patterns with forward rolls. This requires an extreme level of dexterity, so don't rush yourself.

You can play this example while holding down block chords if you like. Pre-place the pick and fingers, then pluck with the pick before rolling forward with the fingers. If you find this a struggle, go back to Chapter Five and refresh your rolling technique with examples 6u–6w.

Again, take ideas like this and apply them to other chord sequences you know. Your goal is to be able to play any triad, in any voicing, across any of the string groups we've covered so far.

Example 7j:

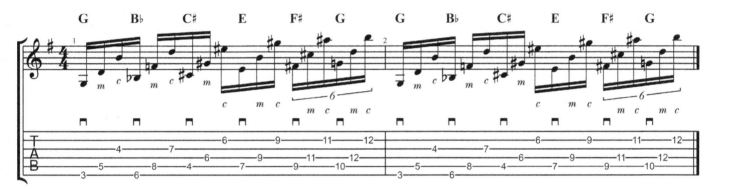

The final set of examples in this chapter teach you the art of *Travis picking* – hybrid style.

While it's common to play Travis style with a thumb pick (or just fingerstyle), lots of guitarists opt to use hybrid picking, so that it can be easily combined with their regular flatpicking style.

In essence, the idea of Travis picking is to combine a picked alternating bassline with a finger plucked chord movement on the higher strings. To build a solid Travis technique we'll start by focusing on the alternating bass pattern only, using a C-shape E major chord.

First, hold down the chord. Now, use the pick and play the bass notes using only downstrokes. The pattern goes fifth string, fourth string, sixth string, and fourth string again. Use your fretting hand fourth finger to alternate between the fifth and six string bass notes.

Work on this picking pattern until it's completely automatic. This is the bedrock of Travis picking and the foundation on which you'll build all melodic ideas. Shortly, you'll need to focus on the melody, so the bass part has to be effortless and happen unconsciously.

It's also good to use some palm muting on these bass part to imitate the sound of an upright bass and help separate the voices when melody is added.

Example 7k:

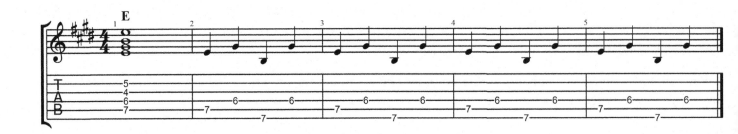

When you've got this movement solid, add a pinch on beat 1 of each bar between the fifth and second strings. Keep the bass muted but let the melody ring out. Check out the audio to hear how this should sound.

Example 7l:

Now add the alternating bassline of Example 7k with a pick stroke on the third string after the low E. Keep the bass part muted while letting the melody ring out.

This might feel new but actually it's the same pinching and alternating motion we've already explored. The only real change is the movement in the bassline. At first, this may feel like you're doing two things at once, but as the bass movement becomes more automatic it will get a lot easier. The key is slow, focused practice.

Example 7m:

Next, I want you to pinch on the 1st beat of bar two and add an additional note on the G string right after, to create a descending roll. The roll is created between the melody and bass parts, and although the goal of Travis picking is to create the effect of two distinct voices, it doesn't mean they can't work together beautifully.

Example 7n:

Another common Travis idea is to pinch with multiple fingers, adding double-stops or triple-stops to flesh out the sound of a chord.

Example 7o:

You can get pretty crazy with these fingering patterns as this ragtime style example shows. There's nothing new here, just an increased amount of syncopation.

Move through each bar and distinguish between notes that are played with a pinching motion, and an alternating motion. This should help you get the sound quite quickly as pinched notes are on the beat, while alternated notes are syncopated.

Example 7p:

With a little practice, these patterns will start to feel natural over any type of chord, as this Rockabilly inspired idea in A showcases. Here you're holding a barred A7 chord at the 5th fret and adding a hammer-on to the G string. As your pinkie is free, you can use that to add a melody note at the 7th fret on the B string.

Example 7q:

How about this open position idea using double-stops with the fingers that screams Scotty Moore on *Mystery Train*? Here, finger the E major chord as you would normally but barre over with the ring finger to hit the double-stop on the 2nd fret.

Example 7r:

For a more comprehensive look at Travis picking, check out my book *The Country Fingerstyle Guitar Method*, and work through it using hybrid picking technique rather than a thumb pick.

As a style, Travis picking can greatly increase your options on the guitar and open up a world of sounds heard in the styles of Tommy Emmanuel, Brian Setzer, Danny Gatton, Albert Lee, Doyle Dykes and countless others. Having solid control of the pick and fingers is an important gateway into applying this to your own playing.

Apply the techniques in this chapter to any chord sequences you know, and spend time focusing on picking smooth basslines while adding the melodic rhythms you've explored here.

In the following three chapters, I've put together some longer performance pieces in different styles for you, which incorporate many of the ideas we've looked at here. Have fun working on them!

Chapter Eight – Prelude In C

J.S. Bach's *Prelude in C* comes from his famed work, *The Well-Tempered Clavier, BMV 846-893* – a series of 24 preludes and fugues written in every major and minor key. While this piece is a masterclass in harmony, we will use it as a vehicle to practice our hybrid picking technique.

Prelude in C moves through a selection of arpeggios that always contain the same groupings of notes: a five-note ascending arpeggio, followed by a repeat of the top three notes.

This can be played in many ways, but hybrid picking provides a wonderfully elegant solution. Every single bar, apart from the final two, should be played with a repeating pattern of,

1) Pick

2) Middle finger

3) Pick, middle finger, ring finger (a forward roll)

4) Pick, middle finger, ring finger (another forward roll)

So that's pick, middle finger, then two repeating forward rolls! This picking pattern includes the occasional bar where the five notes aren't played on adjacent strings.

Although this piece is presented as one long example here, you should learn it in small sections. If you can memorise the chord patterns, the picking hand should take care of itself.

There are a few parts that are worth discussing as far as fingerings are concerned.

In bar five, you need to play an Am/C. Use the index finger to barre the two notes on the 2nd fret, then the pinkie finger to barre the two notes on the 5th fret. The transition to this chord can be tricky, so take your time with it.

The Cmaj7 chord in bar 8 requires you to add the note B before C. Use the index finger for the B, then move it over to the D string for the rest of the chord.

The trickiest chord is the Gdim7 in bar twelve. You'll need to use your pinkie finger for the low G, then index, middle and ring on each fret after. You'll use the same idea to play the Cdim7/G in bar 28.

The Cdim7 in bar 22 will also require a full barre at the 2nd. This barre will then shift up to the 3rd fret for the Dm7b5 chord in bar 23.

Example 8a:

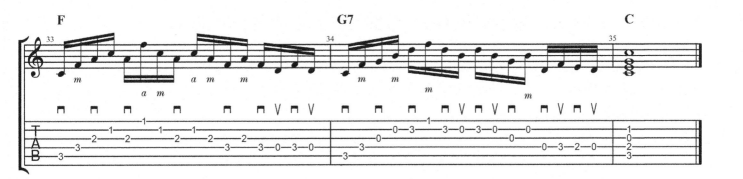

Chapter Nine – Josh Smith-Style Blues

One of the shining lights of modern Blues guitar is undoubtedly Josh Smith. If you haven't heard that name before, I highly recommend you take the time to search out his music – it's a gamechanger!

Born in Connecticut in 1979, Josh has been playing the guitar since the age of 6. Possessing a phenomenal touch on the instrument, he blends his traditional Blues influences, like B.B. King, with Jazz icons such as Charlie Parker, and guitar legends like Jimmy Bryant, Roy Lanham and Danny Gatton.

Combining these influences with a love of authentic '60s Soul and RnB music, Josh's playing is a force to be reckoned with. If the hip players in the '80s had Robben Ford and Larry Carlton to fawn over, we've got Josh Smith!

Listen to his 2017 album *Still* and you'll be treated to a laid back, jazzy blues trio record with a future blues classic in *Charlie's Ray* (an obvious tribute to the legendary Ray Charles). Check out 2009's *Inception* for some more traditional electric blues.

Josh was asked in an interview about the influence of Danny Gatton on his playing. He said, "I couldn't believe what I was hearing from this guy… when I sat down to start to learn anything off this tape, I realised it was physically impossible to do unless I hybrid picked… that quickly became the way I played all guitar."

This chapter contains a swung 12-bar blues in A, similar to how Josh might play it, hybrid picking style. You'll be learning three full choruses here which are broken down into shorter examples for analysis. In the audio download, each part is recorded separately, and there is a performance of the full piece for you to hear everything in context.

The first section of the tune is based around a high register melody that drops down to a riff in the open position and could be considered a kind of call and response idea.

As it's played over an A7 chord, the melody sticks mainly to notes in the A Mixolydian scale.

This section begins by sliding into the 5th fret area with the index finger for a double-stop lick, before moving down to the open position for a riff around an A chord. Finger this A with a barre, this will keep your ring and middle fingers free to be placed down on the 2nd and 3rd frets.

Example 9a:

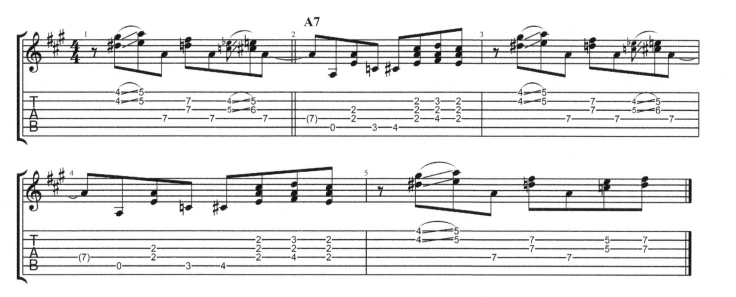

As we hit the D7 chord of the blues, the riff changes to fit the chord, but is still strongly related to the opening theme. Here, use your index finger for the initial double-stop, then slide from the 7th fret A to the 9th fret with the middle finger. This will set you up to barre again on the 7th fret for the following chord punches. As the progression moves back to A7, the riff repeats, as heard in the first example.

Example 9b:

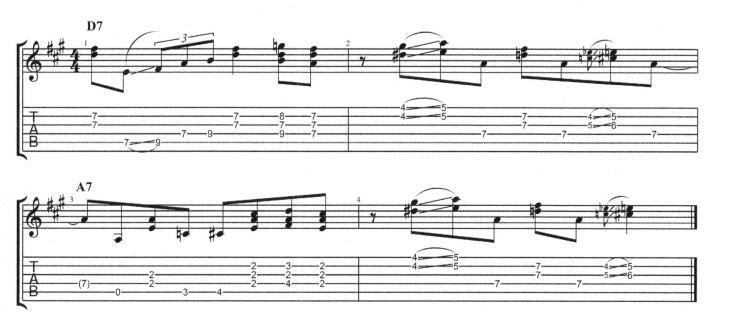

As the progression moves to E7, we summon some *Funky Mama* Danny Gatton vibes with a tremolo picked double-stop.

Tremolo picking is when you rapidly pick a note as fast as possible. This is something you have to use the pick for – a reminder you that hybrid picking can be used in conjunction with the basic guitar techniques you already use.

The example ends with a triplet-based idea before changing the melody that will repeat the next time round the progression, introducing some 6ths to the party.

Use the ring finger for the slide into the 9th fret, and the pinkie finger for the 9th fret high E. Use this fingering to move down to the 8th, then 7th fret, then resolve to the index and middle finger. Take your time with this idea as it will come up again in the next chapter.

Example 9c:

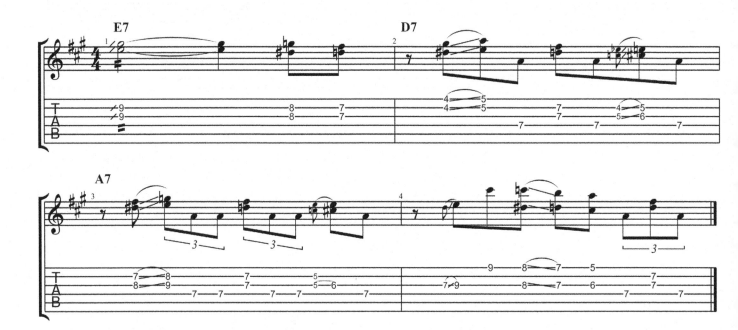

The 6ths melody makes another appearance in the next section and is played against the opening riff. This gives the performance a sense of familiarity without becoming boring.

As with the first loop, the final bar prepares for the move from A7 to D7, this time by taking the 6th intervals and moving them up the neck to the D7 chord at the 10th fret. Use the same fingering as the previous example.

Example 9d:

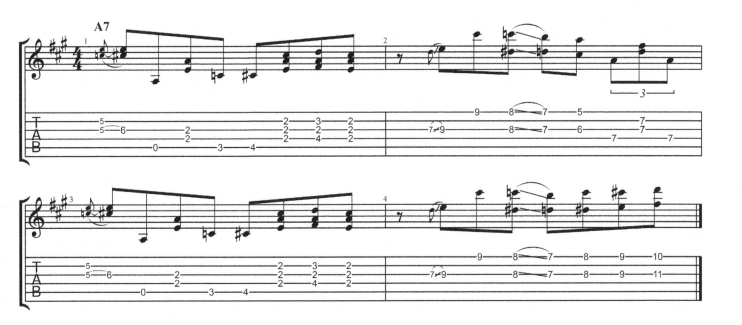

The D7 is outlined with notes from the D Mixolydian scale and is similar to what was played over the A7. We then move back down to the A7 with similar repeating melody and riff ideas.

This lick is almost the same as what was played over the A chord, so use the same fingerings. It should feel familiar, the only difference is that you're up at the 10th fret.

Example 9e:

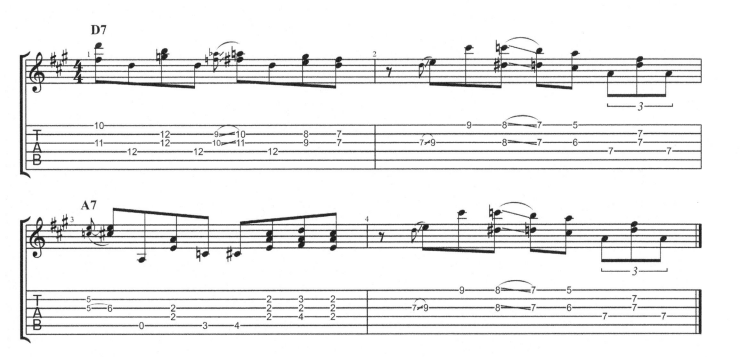

Example 10f repeats the earlier Gatton-style lick over the E7, before repeating the melody from this chorus and the triplet idea from the previous chorus. Next, a new melody is introduced that will be repeated through the final chorus.

You'll be using the same fingerings you used for all the 6ths licks in this chorus. The trickiest part for you here might be the last bar. Perform the slide with the index and middle fingers, then use the ring finger to roll across the 7th fret D and A string. This feels a little more comfortable and is more reliable than trying to use two fingers.

Example 9f:

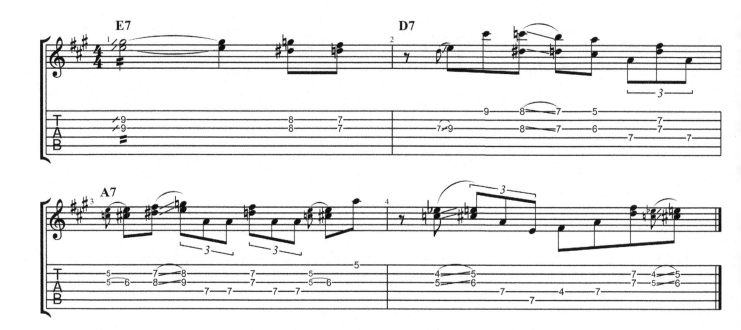

The final chorus varies the riff and continues to alternate between the melody and riff. As with the previous two choruses, the final bar adjusts the melody to prepare for the move to the D7 chord. Finger the lick at the end of the phrase the way you did in the last example.

Example 9g:

A series of 3rds on the G and B string are played over the D7 chord, and these are embellished with some chromatic passing notes. Play these with either two fingers or the pick and middle finger, whichever feels more comfortable.

The melody changes slightly as you lead into the final section, so pay careful attention to both the notes and the rhythm.

For the double-stops at the beginning of the lick, after barring at the 7th fret, you'll play the 9th and 8th frets with the ring and middle fingers. You'll then shift this idea up and down chromatically – don't use different fingerings for each chord.

Example 9h:

The final example features a set of substitutions on the chord changes that you'd expect to find in a Jazz-Blues. This Josh Smith-style blues adds in plenty of ii and IV chords and adds a soulful iv – I resolution found in a lot of post '60s pop.

Not only does this sound great, but it's relatively easy to do. We simply take the melody over the Bm chord and move it up three frets to the Dm chord, before smoothly resolving back to the tonic of A Major. Use a finger per fret for both the Bm7 and Dm7 chords, before resolving to the A.

This idea could be a fingering nightmare if you're not prepared, as there are a lot of position shifts. Take it slowly and focus on where you're going rather than where you are. The secret here is the transition down on the G string. The notes on the 9th, 7th and 5th frets, then the slide into the 6th are all played with the index finger!

Example 9i:

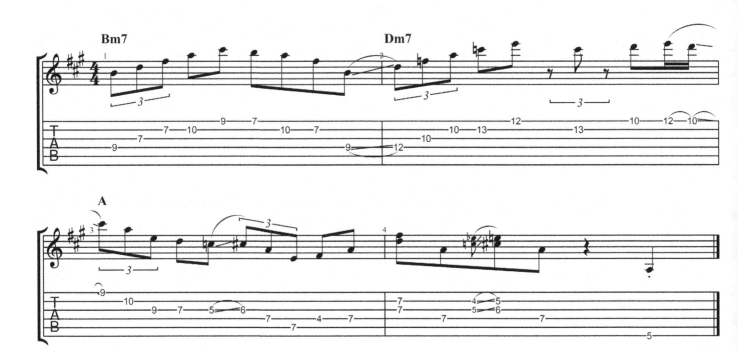

I hope this has given you a little bit of insight into Josh's playing approach and how hybrid picking has helped inform a lot of the music he writes.

If you want to be even more inspired, get yourself on YouTube or Instagram and see what he's all about. Chances are that you've just found your next big influence!

Chapter Ten – Break of the Dawn

Break of the Dawn is a Soul composition by Scottish singer and songwriter, Melisa Kelly. Originally released in 2018 on the album *Devil's Luck*, the song is a heartfelt ballad that uses a selection of Jazz and Soul chord progressions.

When I was given this song to play with Melisa, the first hurdle was that the original recording doesn't feature any guitar – the whole song is played on piano! This meant I had to come up with an arrangement that would work on guitar, but not overshadow the original piano part.

You should now be aware of the musical options hybrid picking offers for a task like this. For me, it became a simple case of working out a nice pattern and applying it to the chord progression.

We're going to learn my arrangement section by section, but the audio recording is of the full performance with Melisa contributing vocals. There's also a backing track minus the guitar, so you can see what it feels like to play some of these hybrid picking ideas with Melisa singing.

The song is played in 6/8 time, so you'll count it,

1 2 3 **2** 2 3, **1** 2 3 **2** 2 3

Listen to the recording and count along to get a feel for this rhythm.

The first example shows the four-bar introduction to the tune, following the same chord progression you'll hear in the verse.

The first chord played is an Aadd11 which has a dreamy quality, but a regular A Major will also work if you struggle with the stretch. Use the index finger on the 3rd fret, the ring on the 6th, and the pinkie on the 7th. This keeps the middle finger free for the bass note on the E string, though you can play this as an open A string if you prefer.

Next, you're moving from the A to a C#m7, then to an F#7#5 which drops down to F#7. Then we go to a DMaj7 and finally a D/E (a D triad with an E in the bass). In Roman numerals the sequence is I – iii – VI – IV – IV/V – I.

The 6th interval lick at the end of the example uses the same fingering you used in the Josh Smith chapter. I play this type of thing a lot and the picking hand fingers make it a lot easier.

Let the notes ring out as best you can – you're trying to fill a piano player's shoes here.

Example 10a:

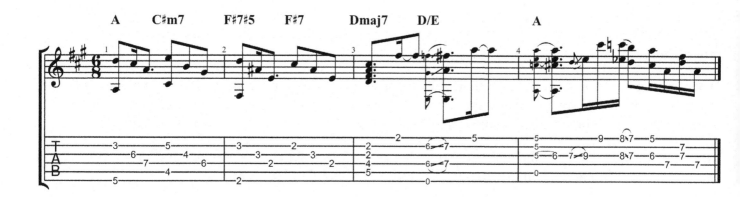

The verse features the same chord progression, but as Melisa is singing at this point, I dialled back the complexity a little. While you may often want to show off what you can do, in a song, your role is to lay down the rhythm and harmony that supports the singer.

You may find the very first chord tricky as you're fretting an Asus2 chord then hammering onto the 6th fret with the ring finger. This requires a degree of left hand dexterity, but the results are worth the effort.

Notice the walk up the scale at the end of the fourth bar. This idea was prominent in the original piano part, so it seemed important to include it. I played it with the pick for maximum definition.

The second four bars contain the same basic chords, but there are some variations in the voicings. While I could easily have repeated the first four bars verbatim, changing the voicings helped the music to feel like it was evolving.

Note the change from A major to A7 in the final bar, which sets up the movement to D major for the pre-chorus.

Example 10b:

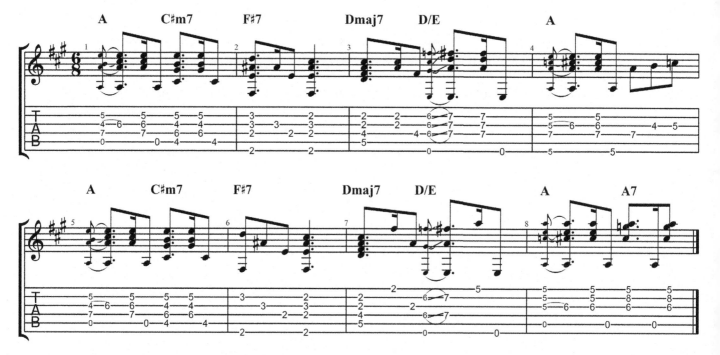

The pre-chorus progression is an interesting one, as it features both a Bm7 and B7 chord. The Bm7 is initially functioning as the ii chord in the key of A, then the B7 acts as a V chord which resolves to the D/E and E7 (which in turn brings the progression back to A for the chorus). The idea at work is a *secondary dominant* (a dominant chord borrowed from another key) to create some harmonic interest.

There's also a C#7 chord in the progression (you'd expect it to be C#m7 in the key of A, as in the verse). This is another secondary dominant chord, this time built on the 3rd degree of the key. This is a popular move in Soul music. Just think of the second chord in Otis Redding's *Sitting on the Dock of the Bay*.

The left hand fingering here should be quite straightforward, though to play the C#7 chord in the second bar will require some strength while you perform a small barre on the 6th fret, while fretting the 8th and 9th.

Example 10c:

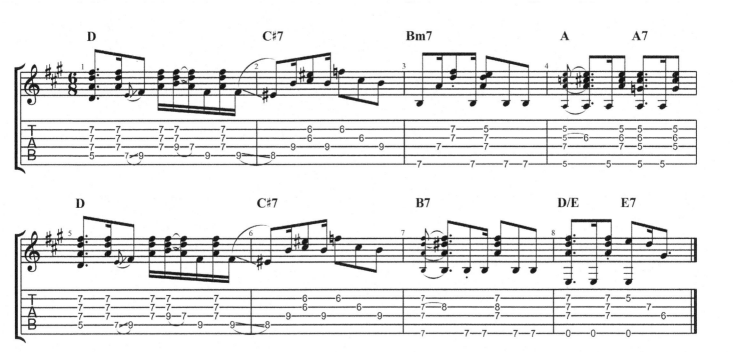

The chorus introduces a wonderful Dm6 chord. This iv minor chord is sometimes referred to as the "nostalgia chord" and it resolves back to the I chord with beauty. You'll almost certainly hear a little slide into that Dm6 as there's a small position shift to navigate there. Don't try any fancy barring on this chord, use all four fingers of the fretting hand.

There's nothing dramatically new in this section of the song, although as a performance it needs to be a bit more intense as it's the chorus, so dig in a little more.

Example 10d:

Between the first chorus and second verse there's a two-bar fill that we get to decorate with some guitar flourishes.

This section begins with a 5th fret A major chord, then moves down the neck with some adjacent string double-stops before ascending again in 6ths.

Example 10e:

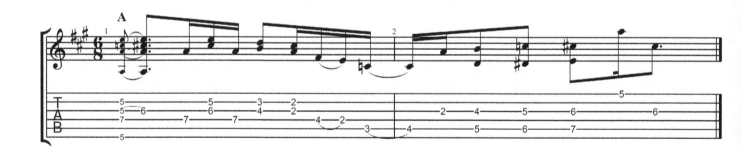

The second verse repeats the chord progression, but again I vary the approach to keep things interesting.

The exciting part is in the fourth bar where we shift up from the 5th fret area to the 9th, allowing us to play the A major and C#m7 chords in a new location.

As with many of the double-stop ideas in this book, you'll be using one fingering then shifting the hand up. So, in bar 4, for example, slide up to the 9th fret with the ring ringer, then finger the double-stop with the ring and index finger. This pattern then moves chromatically up the neck to the A chord.

Example 10f:

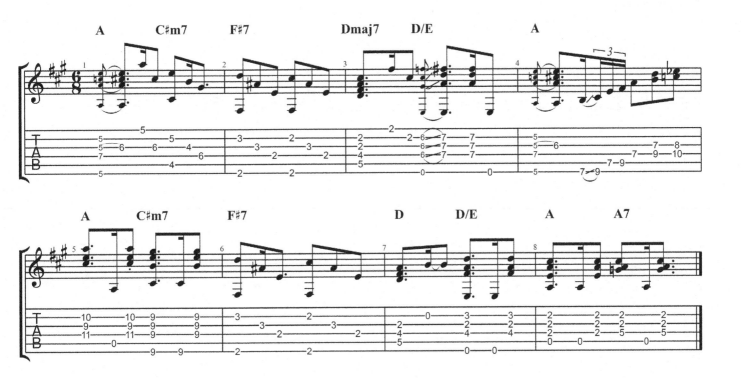

I play the pre-chorus in largely the same way as before, the only difference being the position of the first D major chord, which stops you needing to make too much of a position shift from the A7.

You're covering a lot of the neck here, so make sure you're comfortable with each chord before stitching them together.

Example 10g:

The second chorus is similar to the first, but with the movement from D/E to E7 at the end of the sequence.

Example 10h:

The bridge moves up to the vi chord, F#m7. This alternates with the C#7 chord before moving to D, Dm6 and Bm7, and the perfect cadence into the chorus.

This time around there's a little more emphasis on arpeggiating the chords to create a delicate backing before we go back to the final chord where Melisa opens up vocally.

Example 10i:

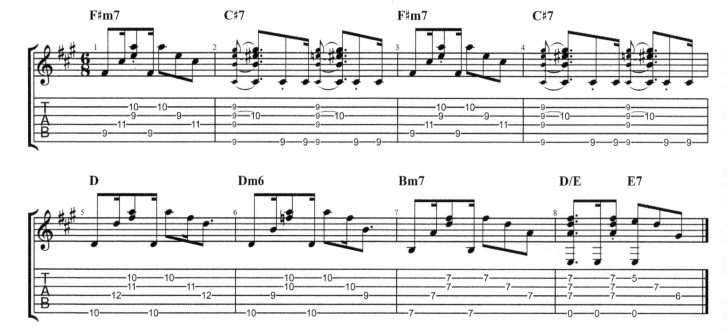

The final chorus begins with a repetition of the second chorus.

Example 10j:

The ending to this chorus introduces a movement that goes from C#7#5 to C#7 to F#7#5 to F#7. These chords are arpeggiated as the top part of each one spells out a melody. You'll be using the same fingering for each of these chords: index, middle, ring, pinkie. The challenge here is nailing the position shift. You should never be looking at where you are, instead, focus on where you're going.

The ending features a beautiful E7b9 chord and I'd normally push and pull the timing a bit here, although I've recorded it in time on the backing track.

Example 10k:

Once you've got all the sections mastered, join them together to play the full song. Listen carefully to the recording and pay attention to my phrasing. I've played the piece straight on the recording, but you'll hear my dynamics.

In a real-world scenario, you'd normally be sitting with the singer, following their cues as they push and pull the time to express themselves. When you've learnt my straight version, why not get together with a singer and give it a try? If you do, please share it with us on Instagram or in our Facebook group so we can show people all the hard work you've put in. Because at this stage… you deserve some credit!

Conclusion

You've made it! It might feel like your journey is over… but it's only just beginning.

Learning a musical instrument is a lifelong process and integrating a new technique into your playing so that it becomes automatic, and also shapes you as a player, can take almost as long. It requires both inspiration from others and your own creativity to find exciting new ideas. But don't hide from new ideas! Explore them, make them your own, be creative, and exploit your strengths on the instrument to find your own voice.

I'm going to finish with a short listening list that includes a variety of players across several genres – all of whom use hybrid picking to some degree in their playing. Check them out and see how they've integrated the technique into their music.

Use this list as a springboard to find players that excite you. A rich musical diet can never hurt, and you can often take ideas from an unfamiliar genre back to your musical home. Music has no barriers or rules, so experiment and have fun!

Who I am – Alan Jackson (1992)

Speechless – Albert Lee (1986)

Junktown – Andy Wood (2019)

Play – Brad Paisley (2008)

Quid Pro Quo – Brett Garsed & T.J Helmerich (1992)

Normal – Bumblefoot (2005)

Solo Guitar Improvisations – Carl Verheyen (2001)

Venus Isle – Eric Johnson (1996)

Introspection – Greg Howe (1993)

Vertigo – John 5 (2004)

Michael Lee Firkins – Michael Lee Firkins (1990)

New Levels New Devils – Polyphia (2018)

Pride & Glory – Pride & Glory (1994)

Tore Down House Scott Henderson (1997)

Signals – Wayne Krantz (1990)

Made in the USA
Las Vegas, NV
11 December 2021